D0355377

A Merry Christmas Herbal

Johnston

A Merry Christmas Herbal

by
Adelma Grenier Simmons

Drawings by Kathleen Bourke

QUILL

New York

Copyright © 1968 by Adelma Grenier Simmons

All rights reserved. No part of this book may be reproduced or utilized in any form or by any means, electronic or mechanical, including photocopying, recording or by any information storage and retrieval system, without permission in writing from the Publisher. Inquiries should be addressed to William Morrow and Company, Inc., 105 Madison Avenue, New York, N.Y. 10016.

Library of Congress Catalog Card Number 68-56414
ISBN 0-688-07080-9 (pbk.)

Printed in the United States of America

12 13 14 15

For all "the Caprilands' Elves,"
my helpers, who make
our herbal Christmas merry

Contents

1
Christmas at Caprilands

Caprilands is our home, a large, comfortable eighteenth-century farmhouse surrounded by fifty acres of fields and woods in Coventry in northern Connecticut. It was built by a prosperous farmer who made a good living from the cattle and horses raised on the pasture land and sold to the West Indies. The name, Caprilands, from *capra* meaning goat, goes back to the time when we raised purebred milk goats on this land. Herbs now cover the rocky pastures, gardens the level meadows, and the old stone walls make backgrounds for shrubs and flowers. But we keep the name for our rugged hilly homestead.

To the north, south, and west our boundaries are trees and meadows; to the east is the roadway, and we welcome our frequent visitors. In winter the strong lines of our colonial house, the sweep of the roofs, and balance in ell and outbuildings are seen against snow-covered fields and gardens. A few hemlocks close to the house break the austere lines and also offer protection to birds. We find all this an ideal setting for the festivities of the "long Christmas" we so enjoy.

But for the early New Englanders, Christmas was a day like any other. The twelve days so richly celebrated in the Old World brought stern disapproval from the Puritans. Many of today's traditions were considered heathen, as indeed they were, for pagan rituals from Greece and Rome, and rites of the Winter Solstice have merged for us with the Feast of the Nativity and Epiphany, the coming of the Magi. Mistletoe, the "golden bough" of classical legend and sacred to the Druids, is still banned in churches, but candles and evergreen wreaths, once part of the ancient Saturnalia, are now acceptable in Christian ceremonies.

Doorway cedars

We begin holiday decorating Thanksgiving week by cutting native cedars to flank two of our six doorways. The trees come from our own fields and those of accommodating neighbors, and the winter red of the wild cedars blends well with our red-brown house. We plant the evergreens in old milk cans painted dark russet and secure the trees against wind and snow with wire stapled to the house. They are regularly watered until spring.

Evergreens, symbols of immortality, have been an aspect of winter festivals from primitive times. Called trees of sanctuary, junipers were believed to have sheltered the Holy Family in their flight, and now they keep from harm all who need help, as the hunted rabbits hiding in the dense pungent branches that mask their scent from hounds. In the Middle Ages, juniper was burned,

or the sap spread above doors, to fend off demons, and junipers
were planted at doorways as protection from witches. Bound by
the devil's law to count the needles before they entered, witches
found the task too onerous and so searched out unprotected
entrances.

With such old tales in mind, we also hang a swag of berried
juniper over each doorway, and embellish the swag with gilded
cones and camel bells.

Birch reindeer

Following a Swedish tradition, we have made a family of
reindeer out of birch logs and branches—two little ones, and
two large ones, antler-crowned.

As Christmas approaches, we provide blankets of evergreens
and herbs, and tie big red bows with bells around their necks.
Placed near the stand of hemlocks across the front of the house,
these primitive creatures of herbal birch are appropriate to this
rustic setting.

To construct a reindeer, select firm birch that will not crack
apart when drilled. Use a good-sized birch log for the body.
Drill holes for four small leg pieces, two on each side, and another
hole at the end to hold the neck section. Saw wood for the leg
pieces into even lengths. Cut a piece for the neck and a short
log for the head. Drill a hole in the head section at one end to
attach it to the neck, and put two holes on top for antlers. Nail
legs, neck, and head in place. Wire boughs together for antlers,
then nail them to the head, fastening the wire tightly to the nails.
Fashion a tail from a piece of bark or a branch.

Bird-feeding wheel

Throughout the holidays, we remember the wild birds. Our
main feeder is a great wagon wheel, fitted with a platform under

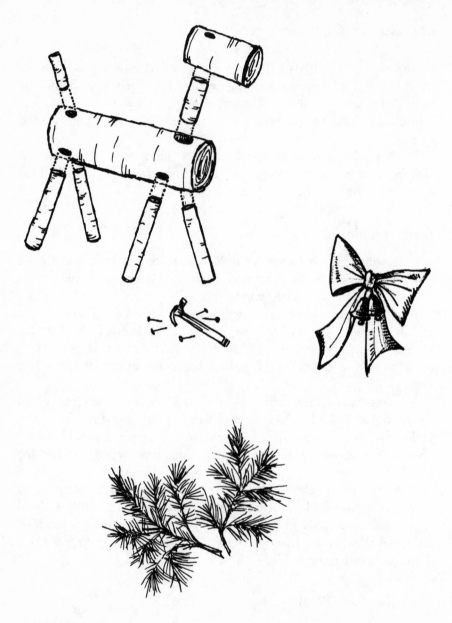

Birch reindeer ready for decorating with a bell-trimmed red bow and an evergreen branch for antlers.

the spokes, and placed on a seven-foot pole that is firmly anchored in the ground. On Saint Barbara's Day, December fourth, we offer a bundle of wheat. On Christmas Day, we tie on small bunches of herbs, gay with bows and glitter—seed-heads of perilla for chickadees, rose hips for robins, and sorrel tops for all the birds. At other times, we offer little bags of raisins and a few large sunflower heads. And all through the year, we keep the wheel supplied with mixed seeds and suet.

Gathering greens and binding garlands

Pine cones are part of the fall harvest. Each year we add new ones to a permanent frieze that encircles our long "keeping room" and runs along under the dark chestnut beams. Cones wired together in three-foot lengths, with cut-cone rosettes at intervals for accent, are nailed and wired directly to the beams and remain throughout the year. For the Christmas season, we drape green garlands behind the cones and let some of the greenery trail down for a festive, verdant look.

Gathering Christmas greens from our own woods has long been a family ritual. For garlands, we collect ground-pine, *Lycopodium complanatum,* a precious evergreen now on conservation lists. Selection from different stands each year keeps our own supply growing. If some is available to you, remember to pull the runners with your foot firmly on the main root; then cut before you reach the parent plant; thus you ensure growth for another season.

There was a time when my father and I would wrest the long green runners from under ice and snow the day before Christmas and spend the night putting up the garlands. My husband, who also enjoys gathering Christmas greens, inaugurated an earlier date, and when my son and his friends came along, we enjoyed a winter picnic in the shelter of hemlocks while we rested on a thick spicy layer of needles. Today my grandchildren share this ritual, returning from the woods decked with greens and looking like Christmas elves.

Ground-pine gathered early is a fine bright green with few brown or yellow sections, and it is easier the first part of December to loosen long unbroken strands. If we make garlands then, the ground-pine stays green all through the holidays. It takes many strands to build a heavy garland. First, snip off any discolored bits; then bind the pieces together with florist wire. Be careful to cover the yellow stems.

Other greens can be used. Cedar lasts well, is readily available, but is prickly to handle without gloves. Laurel from your own bushes (it is also on conservation lists and should not be cut from woods or roadside) lasts well, particularly if sprayed with gold or clear plastic. Small shining leaves of true myrtle, *Myrtus communis,* can be woven into delicate ropes or little wreaths for candleholders. (Culture is given in Chapter 11 on "Growing the Christmas Garden.")

Berries for Christmas

One of the brightest and most enduring reds for fall and Christmas comes from the prolific hedge rose, *Rosa chinensis.* Sprays of red berries, the seed cases or "hips" of the rose, if cut late in fall, provide a fine red decoration. (I prefer them to the orange-toned bittersweet which is not harmonious with other seasonal reds.) Bright sprays wired together hang from our beams and clusters are tucked among brown cones and green garlands.

Mantel decorations

Yew keeps its bright luster even when dry, and we arrange branches on our mantels where other greens quickly lose color in the heat of glowing fires. From the dark beams above the

narrow chestnut mantel of the great kitchen fireplace, we hang
spicy pomanders on ribbons of different lengths. They spin in
candlelight or winter sunshine sending a heady Eastern fragrance
through the room. Also suspended there are hand-carved angels
holding musical instruments, natural-wood Swedish birds, and an
antique wooden duck, its outspread wings freighted with traditional mistletoe and holly.

We decorate another mantel shelf with a dull gold repoussé
Spanish triptych of the Madonna and Child guarded by two
angels; holly leaves, sprayed gold, are tucked among the dark
yew branches that cover the mantel, and gilded pomegranates and
nutmegs are wired to them. At one end stands a miniature antique
chest overflowing with golden balls, cones, leaves, and cinnamon
sticks to represent the gifts of gold, frankincense, and myrrh. At
the other end, figures of the Three Kings are silhouetted against
a shining brass plate. Saint Lucy's golden cat crouches in front
of the triptych, and large rosettes of gold-and-brown cones hang
below with small brass skating lanterns holding holly sprigs.

Some years, to honor Saint Barbara and Saint Nicholas, we
follow a harvest theme and cover the mantel shelf with berried
juniper and sprays of wheat. At each end a wreath of wheat
is hung on the wall. In the center a juniper-framed painting by
a Swedish artist depicts the Wise Men dressed as nineteenth-
century Swedish soldiers. They ride on fine prancing Arabian horses
across a brilliant blue, green, and orange landscape, the trees with
the look of embroidery. Brightly painted roosters from the Prov-
ince of Dala—the cocks that announce the Christmas morning
service—contribute splashes of color. At either end, stand Saint
Thomas candlesticks, traditionally carved in Sweden by peasants
for Saint Thomas's Day, December twenty-first, for the Great
Christmas Fair. Made of pale wood and carved in filigree in the
design of the Cross, each holds two tapers. Black iron candleholders, like swinging Betty lamps, hang from the beams, and on the

floor stands a seven-branched candelabra with gleaming red candles.

At the other end of the room, gilded cherubs support laurel swags above a medieval Virgin and Child. We heap the mantel with gold-sprayed pomegranates and place white-glazed angels among them.

And all through the house

Throughout the house, upstairs and down, we set up small tableaux—in the hall a tiny Christmas tree made on a mesh cone wired with bay leaves, rose buds, and lavender flowers; beside it a nativity scene of carved figures with a crib holding frankincense and myrrh. An artemisia tree stands on an old sea chest of weathered pine. Hung with bright blue birds, bells, and tiny cones sprayed blue and silver, the tree is also decorated with dried blue bachelor's-buttons and delphinium, white and blue statice, and pearly everlastings from the garden. All this associates with our lovely blue-and-white Della Robbia predella which hangs against dark paneling above the chest.

Tableaux and trees combine with our exhibits of dried bundles of labeled herbs hung from rafters, prints of roses old and new, plans for herb gardens, apothecary jars filled with precious gums or the makings of fragrant potpourris, always part of our home. Our special Capriland Christmas trees, designs for holiday tables, and wreaths of many kinds are described in later chapters.

> *The darling of the world is come*
> *And fit it is, we find a roome*
> *To Welcome Him. The nobler part*
> *Of all the house is here, is the heart,*
> *Which we shall give Him; and bequeath this Hollie,*
> *And this Ivie wreath*
> *To do him honour; who's our king*
> *And Lord of all this revelling.*—Robert Herrick

Jesse Tree   *Bird Tree*   *Spice Tree*

2
The Christmas Trees
of Caprilands

Our decorations vary from year to year, but we always place six aromatic cedars, each with a different trimming, at the entrances to the long keeping room—the main room in our farmhouse. Thus we follow an ancient Celtic custom, a pagan practice, of warding off evil spirits through the dark winter months and welcoming the good woodland spirits. Junipers and cedars—both herbal trees—are practical for indoors since they last well and do not drop needles, which is important for a celebration that extends from Thanksgiving to the end of January. We set the freshly-cut trees in deep copper buckets of water and wire them to the russet-painted blinds.

Harvest tree

The Harvest Tree is trimmed with fruit, an early Christmas-tree decoration, when boughs held gifts for hungry children. We select little crabapples that are colorful and keep well. We wire glittering ribbons to the fruits and suspend them along with small baskets and gilt-sprayed cornucopias, both filled with Della Robbia fruits. Straw figures and a Swedish straw star emphasize the harvest theme.

Spice tree

The Spice Tree at the main entrance is trimmed with pomanders gay with ribbons and tiny bells; with spice balls and nosegays of rosemary, rue, and artemisia. Sometimes, for elegance, we wrap the pomanders in gold net tied with gold ribbons. Whole nutmegs and cinnamon sticks on wires, brown gingerbread men in fanciful suits, and frosty cooky stars are hung among bright red and gold foil ornaments, and little bells ring on every branch. On Christmas Eve, we add candy canes and peppermints for our youngest visitors to take home.

Bird-and-flower trees

The Bird Tree of wild juniper is decorated with tiny blossoms of dried sea-lavender, *Statice maritima,* inserted among the thick green needles. We clip on various white birds, including the lovely paper "doves of peace," in a descending curve from tip to lower branches. Little or no foil is used on this tree, which we think of as our peace tree, and it is crowned with a sparkling green-and-silver sequin star.

One cedar is trimmed with red birds, gold ornaments, and bird cookies shaped in Swedish molds. Another is hung with golden ropes of old-fashioned tinsel; gold angels decorate the boughs, a large one at the top. Then there are two big, dark green, pyramidal junipers carrying their natural festive decorations of pink, blue, and gray berries. Some years we add painted ornaments of silver and green.

The Jesse tree

The theme of the Jesse Tree is particularly appropriate to the four weeks of Advent for it is decorated with cards of Biblical quotations that tell of the coming of Christ. These are mainly from Isaiah: "There shall come forth a rod out of the stem of Jesse and a branch shall grow out of his roots . . . and the desert shall rejoice, and blossom as the rose." On one parchment card, wired open for easy reading, we copied these lines in Old English script with illuminated letters; on another a verse from a sixteenth-century hymn:

> *Lo, how a rose e'er blooming,*
> *From tender stem hath sprung,*
> *Of Jesse's lineage coming*
> *As men of old have sung.*

Reflecting the prophecy, we cover branches with handmade roses of red and gold paper, little harps and crowns of gold, a lamb and a dove, and on the tip place a shining star. This recalls the time when Christmas trees were decorated with roses.

Gilded birch tree for children

A birch tree sparkling with gold and glitter stands between sunny windows and is reflected in a long, dark walnut Victorian mirror. Felt and wood cutouts of snowmen, doves, hearts, horses,

and angels shine with sequins. On reachable branches—all ornaments to be removed and enjoyed—are hung spice cookies in
fanciful shapes and homemade candies rolled in foil. Of course,
these decorations must be replaced several times through the
holidays.

To make this tree, we anchor a straight three- to four-foot
birch, or the upper section of a small tree, in a brown crock with
florist clay; this is wedged in the bottom, the crock stuffed with
shredded green florist paper. You might use sand instead with a
layer of pebbles on top. Then we spray tree and crock with gold,
and sprinkle glitter on the branches while the spray is still moist.
You can apply more glitter with Elmer's glue if bare patches
show later.

For an apartment dweller, this small tree is a delight, a festive
substitute where evergreens are too large or prohibited by fire
laws. For the same reasons, the birch is a good choice for schools,
clubrooms, and auditoriums.

Artemisia tree

Small table trees made up of herbal plants, while not spectac-
ular, are fragrant and have an endearing charm. However, a tree
formed by wrapping a wire frame with feathery stalks of artemisia
can be made quite large, say to four feet, if you prefer it to
the traditional fir. We make an Artemisia Tree about fifteen inches
high for an autumn decoration and temporarily replace it for the
twelve days of Christmas with a growing Rosemary Tree.

The Artemisia Tree lasts for several years if a few fresh
branches and a few new blossoms are added each Christmas.
When not on display, it is wrapped in plastic and stored in a dry
place. A quick shower under the spray faucet and careful drying
will freshen it after storage.

For a tree made on a twelve-inch cone of fine chicken wire or

The artemisia tree is a basic design for various other trees. Here it is shown as a wire cone, as a wire cone partly trimmed, and fully decorated as a background for a saint.

metal cloth, you will need a full bushel of *Artemisia albula,* 'Silver King'. (This amounts to cutting down at least twelve established plants.) The artemisia should be well-headed, each white stalk itself a miniature tree. If you harvest in September before seed-heads form, cuttings will dry white; be sure tops are completely developed or they will wilt. You can work while they are still pliable, or hang them upside down in clumps to dry straight.

In addition to the mesh cone, you need a pair of clippers or shears, fine florist wire, and various trimmings—little cones, bitter-sweet or pepper berries, pressed leaves of myrtle (*Vinca minor*) sprayed with gold, or my favorite, dried flowers in muted tones. Yarrow, tansy, everlastings, and orégano blossoms combine nicely with pods of rue and cones of spruce—about two dozen of each. But lime-green sprays of ambrosia with a few colorful dried flowers alone can make a charming herbal tree.

To assemble the tree, first insert the handsomest pointed artemisia spike you have through the wire at the top of the cone. This will establish height. Complete the top by securing six stalks around the first one, pushing stems through the wire.

Next work from the bottom, using long branches if you want a spreading tree. Work upward, slipping stems through the wire cone—tips out and turned up to look like tree branches—until the cone is completely covered and the tree has a pleasing shape. If it is to stand against a wall or on a mantel, you don't need to fill in the back.

I trim the center of the tree with tiny, white, roselike ever-lastings, mingled with bright yellow tansy flowers, the lower part with larger golden yarrow heads. Tucked in at random are pink or lavender orégano blossoms, seed pods of rue, and tiny cones. Only the cones need be attached with wire; other materials will hold if worked into the artemisia branches.

For a true Christmas look, use bright blue birds, little blue and silver bells, and tiny cones. Add dried blue and white flowers from the garden—delphinium, bachelor's-buttons, blue and white statice, and pearly everlastings. Such a tree suggests the legend that on the anniversary of Christ's birth, all trees flowered and all birds sang.

Small half-trees can be made on wire mesh cut into a semicircle and bent to half-cone shape. Once the artemisia branches are in place, such a tree will stand by itself. Of course, half-trees require much less material and space.

Lavender tree

Leafy branches and blossoms make a Lavender Tree of clean penetrating fragrance. It is best designed in July or August when garden plants are fresh and a good supply of true lavender, *Lavandula officinalis,* is at hand. First make the basic Artemisia Tree just described. Then cut twenty-five pieces of lavender foliage, four to six inches long. Insert these among the gray artemisia. Next cut long-stemmed lavender flowers, as many as you can spare from your garden, and press them firmly into the tree, covering all of it except for the top and the tips of branches. In the center of the tree, combine lavender flowers with blue and white statice. This lacks fragrance but offers pleasing contrast to the gray-blue of the lavender. Finally wire small silver bells to the branches and, to give a note of splendor, fasten on a large blue or deep lavender bow.

For an attractive base, use a large round pewter plate, a silver serving tray, a length of lavender or purple velvet, or a piece of gray-blue damask. Or you can introduce pink or fuschia, colors related to the season of Advent.

Rosemary tree

Rosemary, dew-of-the-sea, often blossoms at Christmas with a mist of tiny white, blue, or pale lavender flowers that look like dewdrops on the green branches, hence the common name. A Rosemary Tree is a delight with its shining leaves and aromatic scent. To make the herb look like a tree, select proper plants; I find that those with one root and comparatively broad, dark green leaves make a symmetrical tree that grows in time to some four or five feet. We also make small twelve-inch trees for gifts.

For a large tree, use a twelve-inch pot to give roots ample room to develop; give a feeding of liquid plant food once a month, and water well every day. Also once a month stand the pot in a pail of water that reaches to the pot rim and let stay until the top soils *feels* moist. Mist tops with a bulb sprayer or the spray extension at your sink. Be certain drainage holes are kept open, for rosemary cannot stand wet feet. It must have light but can do without sun during this indoor period. A cool drafty window is fine and away from blasts of hot air. As with most herbs, it releases fragrance when leaves are disturbed or warmed by the sun. Decorate with little bells, stars cut from blue paper, tiny gumdrops, and other candies. Wrap the clay pot, if you wish, in gold, blue, or silver paper.

The Rosemary Tree recalls the journey of the Holy Family and their resting place in a grove of shining fragrant evergreens covered with white blossoms. During the night Mary's blue cloak was laid over one of them. In the morning the white flowers had turned blue in her honor.

Living-herb tree

This is a satisfying little tree to have in a sunny spot through winter. It can be dressed up for Christmas with strands of red cranberries strung on wire or sprays of small rose hips that last so well. A bow of light green and white ribbon sprinkled with glitter and tied around the base, and a silver bell wired to the bow look festive. A friend who shares your enthusiasm for herbs will appreciate such a gift.

For this tree, cut freely from your herb garden as late as November or even the beginning of December, just before you cover the beds with salt hay. These amounts will cover a twelve-inch wire cone:

> 50 pieces of green santolina, 6 to 8 inches long
> 25 pieces of gray santolina, 6 to 8 inches long
> 12 sprigs of rosemary, 6 to 8 inches long
> 12 branches of lavender, 4 to 6 inches long
> 12 sage tops, 4 inches across
> 6 lamb's-ear rosettes, 4 inches across
> 6 horehound tops, 4 inches across
> 12 sprigs of thyme, 6 inches long

Fill the wire cone with wet sphagnum moss and set it on a round black tray, a pewter or pottery plate. Completely cover the cone with alternating lengths of gray and green santolina, thrusting the pieces into the moss. Tuck rosemary cuttings around the base. Then work in thyme and lavender throughout with the lamb's-ears and the sage and horehound tops. These may be wired in place but this is usually not necessary. For another texture, wire clusters of cardamom seeds to the cone.

LEGENDS OF THE TREES

Pine and poplar

When the Holy Family was pursued by Herod's soldiers, many plants offered them shelter, among them, the pine. As they entered a wood to seek the protection of trees, the poplars drew their branches up and began to quake; for their refusal, they must go on quivering forever. But an old pine, hollowed by the years, invited them to rest within its trunk, then closed its branches to conceal them while soldiers passed by. In leaving, the Christ Child blessed the pine, and the imprint of his little hand may still be seen if a pine cone is cut lengthwise.

Long ago, there lived high in the Hartz Mountains a poor widow and her children who gathered cones of the great pine trees to burn for warmth. The day before Christmas, while searching for cones, they were startled by the voice of a little old man, a gay figure who doffed his red cap, sweeping it to the ground. Smiling at the frightened peasants, he said in a merry tone, "Take the cones from under this tree; these are the best." Then with a wave of his cap, he vanished.

They piled the cones in their basket, but when they tried to lift it, it was so heavy, they had to drag it home. That night when they reached into the basket for fuel, they discovered the cones had turned to silver. (And this story is the inspiration for our ceiling frieze of gilded pine cones.)

The fir

This beautiful tree with its aspiring tip was once considered sacred, and sometimes called the Tree of Life. According to legend, it bore blossoms and fruits until Mother Eve picked them. Thereafter the tree grew needles only, but on the night that Christ was born, it bloomed again.

According to a Viking tale, when Christianity came to northern Europe, Faith, Hope, and Charity were sent from heaven to find and light a tree that was as high as Hope, as great as Love, as sweet as Charity, and one that had the sign of the cross on every bough. Their search ended when they found the fir. They lighted it from the radiance of the stars, and it became the first Christmas tree.

Saint Wilfrid is also credited with giving us the Christmas tree. To convince a group of converts that the Sacred Oak, which the Druids feared, had no power to harm them, he brought down the tree with blows from his sharp ax. As the oak fell, it split into four sections, and in the center appeared a young straight fir. Gazing into its green depths, Wilfrid proclaimed, "This shall be a symbol of holiness and peace; it will be the tree of home, for your houses will be built with it; its evergreen will be a symbol of everlasting life. Gifts, kindness, and good cheer shall be sheltered in its branches. This shall be the Christmas tree."

Also from the Hartz Mountains comes an account of an ancient ceremony in which girls danced in a circle around a fir tree while they sang songs, their purpose to imprison an elf who lived in the branches guarding something precious. If he refused to yield his treasure, he would be imprisoned for another year. The tree was richly decorated and also lighted, hence our tree decoration and a carol, too, for translated the song means "to dance in a ring."

Many superstitions cling to the fir: If you would know the length of your life, the fir will tell you; when it is lighted on Christmas Eve, your shadow will be cast on the wall, and if your life is to end that year, your shadow will be without a head. A stick of fir, not burned all through, will ward off lightning. It is bad luck to cut down a fir; in northern countries, wood-choppers so venerated it they often refused to cut it down. In old Russia, when a tree was felled by a storm, it was considered an act of God and the wood was given to the church.

Holly and mistletoe

Apparently the name holly, does not come from *holy* but from *holin,* a name given by early writers. Considered anathema to witches, holly was hung over doorways, in windows, and next to the chimney, lest a witch enter through these openings. The Druids, who venerated the sun, held holly sacred since the sun never deserted its evergreen leaves.

According to Pliny the Elder, it was a plant of many virtues— growing near a house, it afforded protection from lightning and witchcraft; it repelled poison. The flowers caused water to freeze, the wood thrown at an animal compelled it to lie down beside the stick. Whoever first brought holly into the house, husband or wife, ruled for the year.

At first considered a pagan plant inappropriate to Christian homes and churches, holly was later thought to have sprung up under the footsteps of Christ. Its thorny leaves and red berries represented his sufferings. Supposedly the crown-of-thorns was made from holly, and the white berries turned red with Christ's blood.

The word mistletoe comes from the Saxon meaning "different twig," referring to the plant's habit of growing on wood other than its own. Originally, it is said mistletoe was a tree, but when its wood was used for the cross of Christ, it shrank to its present form and was doomed to live on the strength of others.

The companion of holly, mistletoe was also revered by the Druids who taught that mistletoe, too, was holy. Growing in and principally out of the air, it sought the Sacred Oak for support. The cutting of the mistletoe was an elaborate ceremony. Priests dressed in fine white robes and carrying the golden sickle with which the mistletoe must be cut, marched in solemn procession to the Sacred Oak. Beneath it, they spread a white cloth to catch the plants, which must never touch the ground. Two garlanded bulls were then slain under the tree from which the plants were gathered, and their blood fertilized the oak. Pieces of the parasite were distributed among the people to hang over doorways and use as charms to avert fits, epilepsy, poison, tremors, and consumption.

The white berries are sometimes called Frigga's tears for the Norse goddess who grieved so bitterly over the death of her son, killed by an arrow made from the magic mistletoe, that the gods took pity upon her and restored her mischievous son to life. Thereafter mistletoe would be a plant of peace, she decreed, and those who passed beneath it should exchange a kiss.

The hawthorn

The most famous hawthorn, the Glastonbury thorn, was supposedly taken into England by Joseph of Arimathaea who journeyed there to bring Christianity to the ancient Britons. When he paused to rest at "wearyall Hill," he thrust his staff into the ground. There it took root, put out leaves, and blossomed on the birthday of Christ. On this spot the famous Abbey of Glastonbury was built, and here pilgrims came for many years to seek the blessing of the thorn. A scion of this thorn tree was brought to the National Cathedral in Washington, D. C., and now flourishes in the Bishop's Garden.

In another legend, the hawthorn is associated with Christ who rested in a woodland before his crucifixion. There branches of hawthorn concealed him from the soldiers. For this act of love and kindness, the tree was blessed and became one of the holy plants of Christmas.

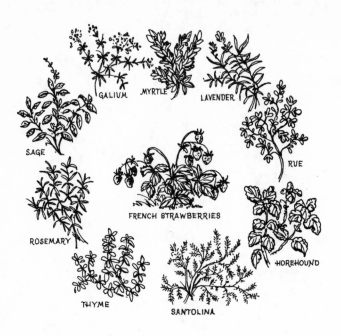

GALIUM MYRTLE LAVENDER

SAGE

RUE

FRENCH STRAWBERRIES

ROSEMARY

HOREHOUND

THYME SANTOLINA

3
Wreaths from
the Herb Garden

Making wreaths for Advent, for holiday tables, doorways, kitchens, and for gifts is pleasant preparation for Christmas. Many of our wreaths are fragrant, for we value the clean fresh smell of cedars mingled with the spiciness of pomanders and the aromas of Christmas baking. Sachets of dried rose petals and lavender fastened to wreaths bring the sweetness of summer to rooms decorated with pungent boughs of juniper, pine, or yew.

Tools

Tools and supplies for wreath-making include heavy 6-, 8- and 10-inch wire rings (a finished wreath will be about 2 inches larger than the ring); a roll of all-purpose 24-gauge silver florist wire; wire snippers—we use one with rounded ends that is easy to carry about; a hand-pruner, kitchen shears, small electric hand drill, rolls of one-inch moss-green and one of cinnamon-brown, or other colored velvet ribbon; and some small clear cellophane bags. To simplify clean-up, spread out a sheet or large dropcloth for a working area. When your wreath is completed, it is easy enough to gather up the cloth and cart off the debris.

Advent wreath of juniper and herbs

The first lights of the season gleam from the candles of an Advent Wreath, a traditional decoration that probably comes from Germany. There, a wreath with four candles—one to be lighted each Sunday before Christmas—was hung in a window for all who passed by to enjoy. It was usually made of wood and decorated with greens; red candles, or more often purple or white ones, were placed in the holders. Each element was significant: burning tapers represented Christ as the Light of the World; purple ribbons and flowers, the penitential aspect of Advent. Pink or rose-colored ribbons and candles sometimes adorned the wreath on the joyful third Sunday, called Gaudete, from *gaudeamus,* Rejoice! Evergreens by their nature suggest life and hope, and the circle is a universal symbol of eternity.

Commercial wooden wreath-and-candle frames now available are not made to hold greens. However, you can wire on a covering of sphagnum moss and insert greens in the wire. But we like to construct our own Advent Wreath and decorate it with materials that will stay fresh through the four weeks of Advent. Ours is designed for a table and placed on a large brass or pewter plate. Any round container, twelve inches or so across and deep enough to hold water, can be used. If it is too deep to display the wreath properly, raise the wreath on stones and tuck in evergreen cuttings to conceal the rim.

My choice of evergreens is the long-lasting, wild Savin juniper, dark on top, silvery beneath and with frosty berries. Beloved of Saint Francis, juniper was traditionally a plant of sanctuary. Yew or spruce would also be suitable but not hemlock, for it doesn't hold up well. Also avoid pine, which is inflammable.

For your wreath, select a circular wire frame to fit your plate or tray. (Wire frames can be bought from garden centers and some florists; ask for a *planting frame* about one inch deep to hold moss and twelve inches across.) Fill the frame with unshredded sphagnum moss soaked thoroughly for easy handling, and secure the moss with widely-spaced lacings of fine wire. At four equidistant points on the frame, press lumps of florist clay large enough to hold the base of twelve- or fifteen-inch candles or slender tapers. Shape the clay into holders and press the candle ends into the clay. Once molded and dried, the clay lasts indefinitely, even in water.

Next insert six- to ten-inch lengths of juniper or other evergreens into the layer of moss, covering it completely. Shape the greens around the frame, clipping the outer edges to make a neat circle. Wrap sparingly with florist wire at necessary points. For another green, use the true myrtle, *Myrtus communis*, a tender fragrant plant from Palestine. Place in the wreath other herbs associated with Advent. Of course, what you select will depend on your garden.

Plants for the Advent wreath

LAVENDER, an herb beloved by Mary, represents purity and virtue. Put a dozen freshly-cut top sprigs into the evergreen and moss.

GRAY OR PURPLE-LEAF SAGE is the herb of immortality and domestic happiness. Flatten it with your hand—the leaves have a tendency to curl—and set at least six clusters about the wreath as points of interest.

HOREHOUND, from Palestine, offers a wish for good health. The frosty white rosettes of early growth associate well with sage.

BLUE-GREEN RUE, a symbol of virtue, supposedly banishes evil and bestows second sight. Arrange it at the base of the candles where it conceals the clay holders.

GRAY-TONED SANTOLINA lasts well and cuttings often root in the moss.

Various other herbs, either as cuttings or plants dug from your garden, could also be included:

THYME, a manger herb and a symbol of bravery. I use it freely through my wreath for it holds its fragrance and cuttings may root.

FRAISE DES BOIS, little French strawberry plants, pushed down into the moss, grow for months if the wreath is watered regularly. Dedicated to the Virgin, these are symbols of true worth.

ROSEMARY for remembrance, and once placed in cradles to protect little children from bad dreams, is the herb that changed its flowers from white to blue in Mary's honor. Pick a number of fresh sprigs to make an inner circle for your wreath. They will root in the wet moss.

GALIUM, Our Lady's bedstraw, is another manger herb from Palestine. Dig small rooted pieces early to put in the wreath; they will make new growth there. Plants in the garden in December are too dry and brown for our purpose.

PENNYROYAL, an aromatic creeper of the mint family, is appropriate, for it was supposed to bloom at midnight on Christmas Eve. To have it look its best, dig small roots and set them in the wreath to produce new plants.

COSTMARY, called Bible-leaf because the colonists placed it as a bookmark in their Bibles, and also known as COSTUS, was the herb used by Mary Magdalen to make the precious ointment. Seedlings or side roots are best.

For color, tuck in various dried blossoms. Dainty, cloverlike pink, white, and purple globe-amaranths are in good scale. They represent everlasting life, as does statice, which has papery lavender, purple, and pink blooms that can be separated into florets. Roadside everlastings provide crisp white accents. And then there are the golden clusters of tansy, also a symbol of immortality. Finally attach small purple velvet bows, and one pink one for the third Sunday, to the base of each candle.

Traditionally, verses from the Old and the New Testament are read aloud and memorized each Sunday as a candle is lighted. On the fourth Sunday all the candles are lighted, the verses recited, and the celebration of Christmas begins. The presence of the Advent Wreath emphasizes the holiness of the season and surely bestows a blessing on the home. This is our prayer:

> *O Lord, stir up thy might,*
> *We beg thee, and grant that by thy protection*
> *We may deserve to be rescued from the threatening dangers*
> *Of our sins and saved by thy deliverance.*

Holly-and-ivy wreath for the punch bowl

Late in winter or early in spring, we fashion a ring of ivy and plant it in sphagnum moss. The ivy grows nicely through the year, with frequent watering, occasional syringing of tops, and an application of liquid plant food about once a month. It is thriving and beautiful for holiday parties and makes a pleasant setting for our punch bowl. (We use a copper one for hot wine and cider; for iced punches, a white Italian pottery bowl with a raised holly design.) Thymes, woodruff, and mints can be worked in with the ivy from time to time, but they do not last so long or grow so well, and need to be frequently replaced.

A metal lid from a barrel or a drum that held grain, tar, or oil makes a good container for the ivy and moss. These lids, less conspicuous painted black or dark green, have depressions around the rims that can hold water and extra plants. Cover the whole surface with sphagnum moss—the long unshredded kind is best—and soak it well before you plant.

Various ivies can be used, perhaps three forms, but no more, and probably none of the variegateds. Green ivies with ruffled leaves are attractive, but we always want some of the familiar English type. Buy plants growing in small pots, since these will have good roots. Remove the pots and push the roots down into the wet moss to cover them. Arrange the plants so leaves conform to the circle. Keep an open center, large enough for the punch bowl, and cover it and any other area where the moss shows, with velvety green moss gathered from some shady spot in spring or fall; it stays green indefinitely.

Early in November, I plant gray herbs along the rim outside the circle of ivy. Cuttings of santolina, sage, lamb's-ears, rosemary, and thyme keep fresh in the well-watered sphagnum and sometimes root by Christmas week, when we replace them with holly sprigs. For the New Year, gilded holly sprays, sprinkled with glitter, and tinsel replace the fresh. But the lovely green ring of ivy remains throughout the year.

Ivy has been associated with wine for centuries. It crowned the brow of Bacchus, the young Greek god of wine—and all his lively followers—for ivy was thought to prevent intoxication. In Elizabethan times, ivy above tavern entrances indicated that superior drink was served. Ivy was then called "the bush," from which came the saying, "Good wine needs no bush." As late as the nineteenth century, a Dr. Fernie wrote, "A decoction of the leaves and berries will mitigate a severe headache, such as that which follows hard drinking over night."

So with a wreath of ivy encircling our punch bowl, we continue an ancient tradition.

Welcome wreath for the Christmas door

An unusual Welcome Wreath for a doorway and a long-lasting Christmas gift is made of ivy plants decorated with sprigs of holly or "tallow berries," which are white, durable berries that come from the West Coast. Fill a circular ten-inch wire frame with well-soaked sphagnum moss. Remove six to eight hardy ivy plants from their two-inch pots and force soil and roots into the moss. Arrange the leaves so that they completely cover the frame; then secure plants and leaves to the frame by wrapping green florist wire around them. If the leaves do not entirely conceal moss and frame, add cuttings of ivy. Then force sprays of tallow berries or bright holly into the moss and complete the wreath with a moss-green and white bow of outdoor weatherproof ribbon.

The ivy will not need water during the holidays, unless the wreath is hung in a very sunny place. When Christmas is over, re-pot the ivy plants and enjoy them indoors the rest of the winter. This wreath offers a different means of giving ivy for Christmas, and brings to mind the familiar carol *The Holly and the Ivy*.

Basic artemisia frame

Many wreaths can be made on a wire frame covered with artemisia. Gather *Artemisia albula*, 'Silver King', in September

when blossom ends are well formed and feathery. (If picked too early, artemisia wilts and shrivels.) Lay stalks flat in an openwork basket, such as an Italian onion basket. Don't hang the stalks, for then they dry in stiff, straight pieces impossible to make circular. For the whitest, most easily-fashioned wreath, work with pliable, freshly-cut artemisia. However, dried artemisia can be shaped if it is hung in an open shed where it absorbs enough moisture from the air to make it supple. You can harvest artemisia, once it is mature, at different times. Late in the season little brown seeds develop, and at this stage, it makes an attractive base for floral wreaths decorated in browns and white—everlastings, brown tansy, and orégano.

For the base of the wreath, shape the stalks of artemisia to the wire circle, breaking stems if necessary. Bind in place with florist wire, looping it lightly to leave space through which you can later push decorative materials.

Separate the good plumes—the silver heads—into two- to three-inch curls, leaving stems long enough to press into the base. Don't use a whole head; it is too ungainly to conform to the circle. For a pleasing all-round design, turn each curling tip toward the center. Shape the inner and outer rims carefully, making edges neat. Keep flat the area between the rims; here you may wish to place a circle of bay or other leaves, perhaps blossoms.

While this wreath is somewhat of a challenge, it can be enjoyed for more than one season, and may even hang from autumn to spring. Then store it in a plastic bag in a dark dry place for summer; in fall, rinse it lightly under a spray of water and let dry in a warm place. Add a fringe of fresh artemisia. Refresh the Herb-and-Spice Wreath (below) with new sprigs of rosemary for greenness and fragrance, replace any spices left from last year, and renew the bow. Little bags of seed herbs wired on for gifts should be used up during the first year.

Mastering the making of the artemisia base is well worth the

Seed-and-sow wreath in three stages with decorations of teasel, chives, camomile, yarrow, brown and green rue pods and a fan of labeled packages of herb seeds tied on with a red ribbon.

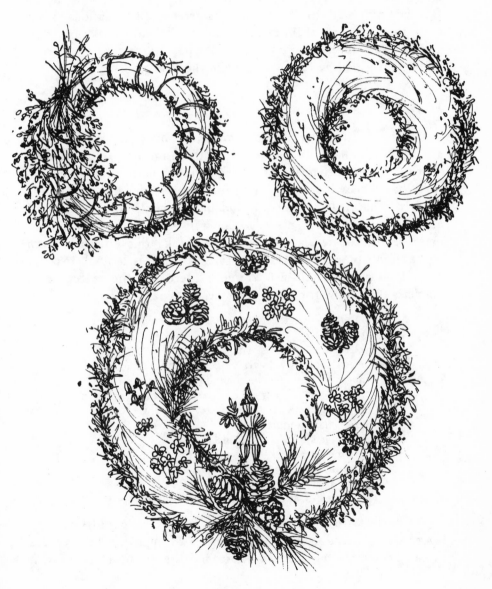

effort, for with it you can create any number of lovely wreaths. In fact, you may want to prepare several artemisia foundations at one time, then decorate them at others. We frequently make up bases a year in advance, using artemisia that has not yet headed since it will be concealed by full plumes from the new crop.

Herb-and-spice wreath for the kitchen

For your Christmas kitchen "workshop" or, again, as a gift for a friend who likes to cook, make this fragrant Herb-and-Spice Wreath on the artemisia base with culinary herbs and spices. Include bay leaves for holiday soups and stews, cinnamon sticks for hot grog, nutmegs for wassail and pies, a circlet of rosemary to adorn a roast, cardamon seeds, ginger root, and mace for Christmas breads, cookies, and coffee-rings. Make this kitchen wreath on an eight- or ten-inch frame. (If wall space is limited, make it on a six- and one-half-inch frame.) Here are the materials in amounts that allow for a few disasters in drilling or wiring.

> 25 to 30 full-length stalks of artemisia, without heavy heads
> 4 well-headed artemisia stalks
> 30 to 36 whole bay leaves (Accumulating enough with unbroken tips may be a problem unless you have a thriving tubbed bay tree, *Laurus nobilis;* then you can also make a handsome circlet for the wreath.)
> 16 to 20 whole nutmegs
> 24 cinnamon sticks, 2 to 3 inches long
> 36 cardamon seeds
> 12 sprigs of rosemary, 3 to 6 inches long
> 2 whole dried ginger roots
>   coriander, caraway, or anise seeds (optional)

Cut florist wire into four-inch pieces. Make clusters of three bay leaves each, inserting one piece of wire through the base of the three. Then wire the clusters all around the artemisia circle with leaf tips turned slightly toward the center to keep the brittle leaves from being broken. (Don't try to wire each leaf to the base, wire in clusters; otherwise you will have too many wires to conceal and too many broken leaves.)

Drill holes through one end (not the middle) of each nutmeg and each cinnamon stick. Wire two nutmegs together, and attach to the base of each cluster of bay leaves. Wire two large or three small cinnamon sticks together and fasten next to the nutmeg. Pierce the base of cardamon seeds with wire and string three together; add to each bay cluster. Force pungent green sprigs of fresh rosemary into each grouping. Cover any exposed wire with additional artemisia.

If the wreath is to be a gift, make up little transparent bags of coriander, caraway, or anise seeds for Christmas baking. Tie them to the bottom of the circle with a velvet bow and wire a nutmeg to this. Drill ginger roots and wire them to the wreath on each side of the bow just above the seed packets. Hang with bow at base.

Fragrant wreath of flowering herbs

A wreath to be decorated with dried flowers, seed pods, and cones requires a full lacy base and more artemisia is needed than for the kitchen wreath. Follow the directions given above for making the artemisia base but use more of the showy white curls throughout. Before decorating, hang up the wreath to check shape from every angle and to add more artemisia if necessary.

Here are suggestions for a ten-inch Fragrant Wreath of varied colors and textures. If you gather blossoms of the same herb at different times, you will have many delicate shades to work with. I seldom use all these listed below in one wreath—though they would certainly make an attractive one. I often select materials in whites, browns, and grays, using pale yellows for accent, as everlastings, brown orégano, and the last blossoms of tansy. It helps to lay materials on top of the artemisia to develop the complete design before you weave them permanently into the base.

TANSY dries bright yellow to brown and looks gay throughout a wreath. You need one to two dozen flowers.

ORÉGANO has early blossoms of bright green, purple, and pink, depending on variety; later they are brown, and all are fragrant. Dry at different stages to get contrast. Use one to two dozen in random fashion.

EVERLASTINGS, those from the roadside, picked in the middle of September are white with a fluff you can shake off outdoors; later blossoms are creamy yellow and look like tiny daisies. They need to be massed to look well, so pick a full bushel. As a frame for brighter blossoms, we frequently make a circle of everlastings at either the inner or the outer edge of the wreath.

GOLDEN YARROW is a glowing addition to any wreath. The full heads of most varieties are too large, so break them into sections and space about six around the wreath.

WHITE YARROW, *Achillea millefolium,* also makes good accents.

GOLDENROD, particularly the early lanceleaf type, looks like mimosa and does not carry the heavy pollen of later varieties. Little sprays are sprightly notes in a design.

STATICE in yellow, orange, and white contributes a delicate texture. *Statice sinuata* is brittle but beautifully colorful and *S. maritima* is white, pliable, and easy to work with.

AMBROSIA, *Chenopodium botrys,* with lime-green plumes adds much to a wreath. If used when green and sticky, it sheds very little.

Be wary of strawflowers. Their intense colors may overpower the muted tones of your herbal flowers. The tiny home-grown type with subtle shades is usually preferable to the showy commercial kind.

For sculptural interest, use groupings of the beadlike seed pods of rue, chartreuse when they first develop, later a warm brown; also very small spruce cones; red-brown sorrel seed-heads and those of the wild St.-John's-wort, *Hypericum perforatum*. Harvest the sorrel in August before the white-flecked heads shatter, and hang up to dry; then break into usable segments. Only small pieces of dock look well; also break the large dark-red blossoms into sections.

As with other artemisia-based wreaths, this Fragrant Wreath can be stored in a bag through spring and summer, freshened with a spray of water in fall, and refurbished then with some new materials for repeated enjoyment from year to year.

Victorian wreath with fragrance

Of the many wreaths that bring a summer garden to a winter home, this Victorian Wreath seems to me the most delightful. Our design was suggested by nineteenth-century prints, and also by my recollection of a faded wreath under glass in my grandmother's parlor. Delicate hues of pink rosebuds and lavender blossoms predominate, but the wreath is made on the same pearly background of artemisia. The sweet-smelling assemblage includes thymes, orégano, ambrosia, lavender, rosemary, everlastings, statice, and globe-amaranths.

First make the basic artemisia wreath on an eight- or ten-inch wire circle. Then develop your design, placing the floral materials before pressing them into permanent position. For a colorful, fragrant wreath you will need these approximate amounts of dried blossoms:

> 30 to 50 rosebuds, pink. Push a stiff wire through the thickest part of the rose near the stem; then make

clusters of buds. For our wreaths, we use rosebuds
imported from southern France; they are solid and
take wire without breaking. If you decorate with
small rosebuds from your garden, preserve them with
clear plastic spray for they are likely to be fragile.

12 lavender spikes for both color and fragrance; use
more if you wish. Cut early, as soon as blossoms have
color; dry in a basket, heads-up.

For more fragrance and also for textural interest, include:

   6 orégano blossoms
   6 rosemary sprigs, still green
  10 thyme sprigs with lavender blossoms
   5 or 6 pink hydrangea florets to be placed around the
      circle
   6 ambrosia sprigs at least—12 to 15 if you have that
      many. Pick this green and place while fresh so that
      they will hold color and be less likely to shatter. Am-
      brosia, too, gives off a delicate fragrance.
  12 sprigs *Statice sinuata*—pink, lavender, and blue—for
      color. (This is brittle and scarce.) Or substitute 12
      sprigs *S. maritimum,* sea-lavender.
  25 sprigs of everlastings for delicate flowery texture

After you have worked out your design, first force the most
abundant materials into the artemisia base. Make a complete circle
of everlastings. Perhaps place *Statice sinuata* as accent, and make
a circle of *S. maritima.* Push wired clusters of rosebuds into the
artemisia, then insert the lavender, hydrangea florets, and blossoms
of orégano, rosemary, and thyme. Because ambrosia is brittle, press
it in at the last.

Leave space at the bottom of the wreath for bows and two small
bags of sachet. For these cut 6-inch squares of pink and lavender
netting or organdy. Put one-quarter cup of rose potpourri in one
square and the same amount of lavender in the other. Shape into
balls about the size of a crabapple, tie with a twist of wire with ends
long enough for fastening. Wire the sachets to the wreath. Flatten

and fluff out the net and cut off any excess. Wire bows of pink and lavender velvet ribbon to the top of the sachets, where they join the wreath, and decorate each with a rosebud cluster, a drop of rose oil on each bud. A few small rose-geranium leaves, tucked in while green, add a compatible fragrance.

Wreath of lavender

This variation on the Victorian Wreath is made principally with leaves and blossoms of lavender which grows in abundance at Caprilands where plants usually bloom twice in a season. If you also have a plentiful supply, you might make up several of this clean-smelling Lavender Wreath for Christmas gifts.

Start with the artemisia base. Insert enough fragrant leaf cuttings—before they dry out—to completely cover it. Decorate with lavender flowers, picked at peak and inserted while fresh. Complete your wreath with colorful groupings of lavender, purple, and white statice, which will help to fill out the wreath.

Then make a sachet of lavender blossoms tied in lavender and green net; wire it to the wreath. Lavender, white, and green ribbons complete this pretty ornament whose fragrance is indescribably delightful. You can wire on small bags of lavender decorated with nosegays and bows all around the wreath, and remove them from time to time to bring fragrance to closets and drawers.

Seed-and-sow wreath

This wreath offers a pleasant way to share the wealth of your garden with a practical gift for a new herb enthusiast. Prepare the dried artemisia base on a wire frame. Then cover it with green ambrosia. Insert seed-heads of garlic-chives, brown-and-green rue pods, dried yellow tansy heads, and dark brown orégano. Decorate with bunches of daisylike camomile flowers, and some lovely, fragrant *Artemisia annua* that dries dark brown and is very decorative.

At the bottom of the wreath, wire on a fan of labeled packages of herb seeds, each with a card giving culture and use. Finish with a ribbon bow and place the wreath at once in a plastic bag. This perishable wreath must be handled with care or the seed-heads will shatter.

> *A chaplet me of herbs Ill make,*
> *Than which tho' yours be braver,*
>   *Yet this of myne Ill undertake*
> *Shall not be short in savour.*—Michael Drayton

HERTHA

GODDESS OF THE HEARTH

4
Hertha and Huldah,
Fire and Flax

At Caprilands we celebrate every shining facet of the glorious Christmas season. Knowledge of legends, rituals, and plant lore increases year by year. We learn from old herbals, calendars, prints, and books, and also from enthusiastic guests who attend our festivals and share with us their own Christmas customs and recipes. Thus our celebrations are based on those of many lands and many centuries.

The festivals of the month before Christmas reflect pagan as well as Christian rituals, for ancient practices have been merged with modern celebrations. The days leading up to the Winter Solstice on December twenty-second are the still dark days in our year; life for the time seems dormant, the sun at its farthest point from the earth. We feel the need to bring light and warmth to this cold period, and it is with some ceremony that we put a match to the first fire of December at Caprilands. As dusk falls, we touch a flame to kindling and candles, and by fire- and candle-light enjoy the pungent fragrance of fresh evergreens and rosemary, and the sweet spice of newly-made pomanders. Piled by the hearth in a woven basket are faggots made from herbs no longer useful as seasoning or decoration. As we burn these fragrant offerings, we recall many legends.

Hertha of the hearth

Hertha, as her name implies, was a Teutonic goddess of the hearth. In the days when houses had no chimneys but only a roof opening to let out smoke, an altar of stones stood in the center of the great hall. When flames were liveliest from pitch pine, fir, and sweet juniper, Hertha would appear, her hair coils of smoke, her shoes glowing coals, her long face dominated by a great iron nose. Although she was homely, she was a source of warmth and inspiration for those who worked by her flame through the dark winter. She encouraged singers and bards, spinners and weavers of flax. She was also a fortune-teller and a bearer of gifts—a joy to good children but a terror to the unruly. It was in her power to bestow health, beauty, and virtue. Dough, baked in the shape of little shoes, was set out to receive her offerings.

The burning of aromatic juniper branches and berries was a pagan rite to drive off witches, and the devil himself, with flames through the twelve days of Christmas. On Christmas Eve and New Year's Day, children marched through the streets carrying poles topped with bundles of burning herbs and juniper, while drums beat, bells rang, horns blew, and whips cracked—all measures to ward off evil spirits through the holy days.

Huldah, the weaver

Huldah, from the Tyrolian Alps, an earth goddess, taught mortals how to weave with flax. In summer, she visited the fields to observe the gathering of fruits and grains. In winter, she came to the fireside to check whether the housewife was making thrifty use of the harvest.

Flax is an herb rarely grown today except for the beautiful perennial type. Its many ancient uses are almost forgotten, but *Linum usitatissimum,* from which both linen and linseed are made, was so important that Pliny the Elder asked, "What department is there to be found of active life in which flax is not employed? . . . What audacity in man! Thus to sow a thing in the ground for the purpose of catching the winds and tempests, it being not enough for him, forsooth, to be bourne upon the waves alone!"

Flax has many practical uses for cords and sailcloths, lampwicks, seedcakes to fatten cattle, oil for polishing, and in the fresh state, medicine. Historically, fine linen clothed the living and the dead from Egypt to the British Isles, and the clear blue flowers were a protection against sorcery. In Germany, it was believed that a sickly child could be made well if he was placed naked on the grass and flax seed was poured over him. The seed was left to grow, and as it flourished so supposedly did the child. In Bohemia, seven-year-olds danced through fields of flax in order to become beautiful.

Our own use of the little nodding heads of *Linum perenne* and *L. usitatissimum* in dried arrangements began some years ago. Honoring Huldah at Christmas, we make an exhibit of flax in our upstairs library. It includes a fine old flax wheel, discovered in the barn, and also a hatchel—an alarming wooden implement with iron spines through which flax was drawn to remove coarse fibers.

Beside wheel and hatchel, we place bundles of dried herbs and an illuminated volume with the legend of Huldah. No picture of her could be found so she is represented by a bow made from a red-bordered, homespun towel. Over the mantel, we hang a spinning wheel wreathed in evergreens dotted with shining flax pods. Sometime before Christmas we have a party to honor these two favorite goddesses—Hertha of the Hearth, and Huldah, the Weaver.

Recipes for Hertha and Huldah party

HOT CIDER PUNCH

1 gallon sweet cider
4 cinnamon sticks
1 slice fresh ginger
12 cloves

4 oranges, quartered
2 quarts cranberry juice
Sugar to taste
Extra cinnamon sticks

Simmer cider with the spices and oranges for 1 hour. Then add the cranberry juice and sugar to taste. Serve hot in pottery mugs with cinnamon sticks as stirrers. Makes 6 quarts.

SAFFRON RICE WITH SEAFOOD

¼ pound (1 stick) butter
2 tablespoons oil
4 green peppers, finely chopped
2 cups chopped celery
2 onions, finely chopped
1 pound chopped mushrooms, *or*
3 6-ounce cans broiled-in-butter
mushrooms
1 cup chopped pimiento
1 cup tuna chunks
1 cup crab meat
1 pound frozen cooked lobster,
cut in pieces

1 teaspoon salt
1 teaspoon saffron, steeped 10
minutes in 1 cup boiling water
1 10½-ounce can cream of celery
soup
1 10½-ounce can cream of chicken
soup
2 pounds white rice, cooked
Chopped stuffed green olives, parsley, paprika

Melt butter and oil in a deep iron skillet or flameproof casserole.

Remove seeds and ribs from green peppers, chop and sauté with celery and onions for a few minutes, then add mushrooms; stir and brown. Mix in pimientos and seafood and salt. Combine saffron and water with creamed soups. When thoroughly mixed pour into casserole with vegetables and seafood. Stir in cooked rice, garnish with chopped olives, parsley, and paprika. Place in a 350-degree oven, covered, to heat through, about 25 minutes. (*Note:* Always soak saffron in boiling water or other liquid at least 10 minutes.) Serves 25 generously.

CAPRILANDS FAVORITE CHRISTMAS COOKIES

Along with the many traditional cookies that are hard and chewy, we like this favorite recipe of my mother's, a soft spicy cooky that, kept properly in an airtight tin, stays fresh for weeks.

½ cup shortening	2 tablespoons whole anise
½ cup sugar	1 tablespoon ground coriander seed
½ cup molasses	1 scant teaspoon ground cloves
1 egg (unbeaten)	¼ teaspoon salt
2¼ cups flour	2 teaspoons baking soda
2 teaspoons ground ginger	2 tablespoons hot water
1 teaspoon ground cinnamon	6 tablespoons strong black coffee

Cream together shortening, sugar, molasses, and egg. Sift flour, spices, and salt together. Add to the shortening mixture. Dissolve soda in hot water and set aside. Add coffee to flour-spice mixture. Beat in soda. Mix well, drop by spoonfuls onto a greased baking sheet, about two inches apart. Bake in a 350-degree oven approximately 15 minutes. Do not overbake as cookies should stay soft. Yield: about 60.

Sherry Frosting: Stir 3½ tablespoons of sherry into 2 cups of confectioner's sugar and spread over cookies. Decorate with colored sugars, halves of cherries, bits of angelica. The frosting stays white for just two days, so ice cookies only as you can use them.

CURRIED CORN SOUP

¼ pound (1 stick) butter
1 tablespoon curry powder
1 teaspoon powdered freeze-dry shallots
2 1-pound cans cream-style corn

1 1-pound can whole corn
2 cups medium cream, warmed
⅛ teaspoon ground rosemary
2 tablespoons chopped chives

Melt butter in pan, add curry, stir until smooth. Add shallots, then corn, stirring slowly; then cream and rosemary. Garnish with chives. (Evaporated milk or "half-and-half" may be substituted for medium cream.) Serves 8.

CAPRILANDS HERB BREAD

½ cup sugar plus 1 teaspoon
1 tablespoon salt
⅓ cup butter
2 cups boiling water
¼ cup lukewarm water
2 packages dry yeast
2 eggs

2 tablespoons Caprilands Mixed Herb Seasoning
2 tablespoons chopped parsley
¼ cup chopped pimientos, well drained
8 cups unsifted flour
Butter to rub on hands

In a large bowl, dissolve ½ cup sugar, salt, and butter in boiling water; let cool to lukewarm. In a 1-cup measure put ¼ cup lukewarm water, the remaining 1 teaspoon sugar, and the yeast; let yeast bubble until it fills the cup. Add to the sugar, salt, and shortening mixture. Beat eggs until foamy and combine with mixture. Stir in seasoning, parsley, and pimientos. Add 4 cups of unsifted flour; beat until smooth. Gradually mix in the 4 remaining cups. Turn dough out on a floured board and knead until all is well combined. Place in a greased bowl, cover with waxed paper, put in refrigerator, let rise for 3 hours. Remove at the end of this time, cut dough into three parts, rub hands with butter, knead the dough well until all air is removed, shape into three large loaves. Place in well-greased pans, lightly cover, and let rise in a warm place for 1½ hours. Bake in a preheated 350-degree oven for 15 minutes, reduce heat to 300 and bake another 30 minutes until loaves test done. Cool in pans on racks, then remove from pans. Do not cut for several hours. Yield: 3 large loaves.

An excellent bread with turkey or for turkey sandwiches. Its appearance is gay, in keeping with the season, and the piquant taste is a pleasant change from the sweet breads of this time.

Note: Caprilands Mixed Herb Seasoning is ground and easy to combine. You can substitute a good poultry seasoning, or a mixture of ½ teaspoon rosemary, ¼ teaspoon thyme, 1 teaspoon savory, ½ teaspoon sage, and a pinch of garlic powder.

> *And here I brew both ale and wine,*
> *Now fire and hot meates have thou must,*
> *December loves warme potions.*
> —Ram's *litte Dodoen,* 1606

SAINT BARBARA

5
Saint Barbara's Day—
December 4

The Feast of Saint Barbara is the first festival of the Christmas season at Caprilands. Her legend had its beginning in the East, and she is still a familiar figure throughout the Near East and Asia Minor. Relatively unknown in England, she is the patron saint of Ferrara and Mantua in Italy.

Barbara is supposed to have lived in the third century. Her father, Dioscorus, a pagan Greek of great wealth, imprisoned his beautiful daughter in a tower to protect her from the world. In her solitude, she was secretly converted to Christianity and baptized.

Saint Barbara's wreath in three stages. Decorations associated with the harvest include wheat, pine cones, rose hips, garlic blooms, and a straw figure representing the Saint.

While her father was on a journey, she added a third window to her tower to symbolize the Trinity. For her refusal to practice pagan rites, she was tortured and finally put to death by her own father whom lightning instantly destroyed.

Saint Barbara is a protector against lightning, fire, storm, and sudden death; and, by analogy, patron of armorers, gunsmiths, and artillerymen. Her customary emblem is a tower. She is also depicted with a book, a cup representing the sacraments, a palm, symbol of victory, a sword for martyrdom, a crown, wheat for the bread, and a rose for the miracle of substitution.

In Syria, Saint Barbara's Eve was celebrated as a masquerade. Children, in fantastic costumes visited from house to house, singing, asking for a blessing and gifts of decorated eggs, coins, or candies made of wheat. Wheat in various forms was displayed in this final harvest festival of the year for which baklava and other pastries baked in traditional molds, and sweets of wheat, sugar, and rose water were prepared.

As a beautiful and courageous figure, Saint Barbara became an inspiration to young girls. Her day was celebrated with fortune-telling; in her honor, they forced fruit-tree branches to blossom at Christmas, competing with each other to have the largest blooms. If a young man stole a branch from a girl's bouquet, he was likely to become her husband.

Saint Barbara was associated with the harvest, and wheat is often her symbol, although other plants bear her name as *Barbarea vulgaris* or winter-cress, *herbe de St. Barbe,* and *barbenkraut.* A popular custom was to sow grain in moss in two plates, watering it until sprouts appeared. The percentage that grew was indication of the next harvest, the angle of the sprouts, the direction of the prevailing winds.

Festival decorations

Honoring the legendary Saint Barbara, we develop a harvest

theme for her day and include her various symbols. We arrange long sprays of wheat in a wooden mortar, and gild and rub a sickle with raw umber. A sword, a chalice, a palm, and a painting of the Saint with her tower identify her legend. On the table, bowls of puffed wheat represent the Syrian dainties. Outdoors we raise a sheaf of grain to the birds on the great wagon-wheel feeding station and wire a shock of corn there for both food and shelter. Wheat and golden roses decorate our mantels.

Recipes for Saint Barbara's Day

Our recipes for this feast day are of Near Eastern inspiration, modified to our taste. Main dishes are garnished with mint leaves, sesame seeds, Barbara's cress, and there are cakes with candied rose petals. We decorate each table with a spray of wheat and a bowl of puffed wheat made into the Syrian dainty by sprinkling with rose water, tossing in vanilla-flavored sugar, and spreading out on a cooky sheet to dry in a 100-degree oven for about 15 minutes.

CAPRILANDS VODKA PUNCH

1½ cups lime juice	1 cup mint leaves
2¼ cups lemon juice	1 quart vodka
2 cups sugar	1 gallon dry white wine
1 small leaf wormwood	Mint sprigs

Strain the lime and lemon juice and combine with the sugar. Place in a blender with wormwood and mint leaves. Blend at high speed until leaves are finely ground. Pour into a punch bowl containing a cake of ice, and add vodka and white wine. Garnish with sprigs of mint. Yield: about 48 servings in 4-ounce punch cups.

SESAME CHICK-PEA SPREAD

This spread is made with a sesame paste called *taheeni* or *tahini*, which has the consistency of peanut butter. It is available in tins in

Near Eastern grocery stores and some specialty shops. A similar preparation called Chi-Chi-Dip can be purchased and needs only the addition of a little lemon juice.

1 cup canned chick peas	½ teaspoon salt
1 cup sesame paste (*taheeni*)	1 clove garlic, crushed
½ cup lemon juice	¼ cup olive oil

Simmer the chick peas in a little water until soft; then mash or purée in the blender. Mix in the sesame paste combined with lemon juice. Beat with a whisk or fork and add salt, garlic, and olive oil. Serve as a dip, or spread on dark whole-wheat crackers topped with sesame seeds. Makes 2¾ cups.

CHICKEN ROLLS

1 12-ounce can chicken	Salt to taste
½ cup chopped candied ginger	Freshly-ground pepper
½ cup ground almonds	2 teaspoons lemon juice
1 teaspoon freeze-dry shallots, pulverized in a mortar, *or* 2 fresh shallots, minced	4 tablespoons butter, softened
	1 8-ounce package cream cheese
2 teaspoons curry powder	¾ cup sesame seeds
	1 tablespoon sugar

Chop the chicken very fine. Crush ginger in a mortar. Combine remaining ingredients (except sesame seeds and sugar) with the butter and cream cheese. Toast sesame seeds with sugar in a heavy iron pan or skillet (no oil is necessary) over medium heat. Stir with wooden spoon for about 5 minutes. Seeds should be crisp but not dark. Let cool. Shape the chicken mixture into four rolls. Cut waxed paper into pieces, each big enough to hold one roll. For each roll, sprinkle 2 tablespoons of toasted sesame seeds on the paper and roll the chicken in the seeds until thoroughly coated. Twist ends of paper together, wrap rolls in foil, and store in the freezer. When you are ready to use them, bring rolls to room temperature and serve with sesame-seed crackers. About 35 servings.

LAMB CURRY WITH FRUIT
To be served on hot cooked white rice.

Part I, Roast Lamb

5-pound leg of spring lamb
1 clove garlic, crushed, *or* ½ teaspoon powered garlic
1 teaspoon dried thyme
½ teaspoon dried rosemary

½ teaspoon dried orégano leaves
1 teaspoon salt
½ cup (1 stick) butter or mar-
garine
1 cup white wine

Place the leg of lamb on a sheet of aluminum foil large enough to wrap around the meat. Blend the garlic, herbs, and salt into the butter and rub the mixture over the lamb. Pour on the wine. Wrap the foil tightly around the meat, sealing the edges. Bake in a 400-degree oven for 2 hours.

Part II, Curry Sauce with Fruits

4 shallots *or* 1 onion, sliced
¾ cup (1½ sticks) butter
3 teaspoons curry powder
6 tablespoons flour
2 cups chicken broth
1 bay leaf
2 tablespoons chopped parsley
¼ teaspoon dried thyme

½ cup rosemary or other tart jelly
2 teaspoons lemon juice
1 teaspoon grated lemon rind
½ cup grated coconut
Salt and pepper to taste
4 bananas, peeled and sliced
2 apples, pared and chopped

Sauté shallots or onion in ½ cup of butter for 5 minutes. Add curry powder and flour. Cook, while stirring with a wire whisk or wooden spoon, for 3 minutes. Slowly pour in the chicken broth while stirring. Then add bay leaf, parsley, thyme, jelly, lemon juice and rind, and coconut. Cook and stir for 5 minutes, then add salt and pepper to taste.

In a separate pan, sauté bananas and apples in the remaining butter for 5 minutes; then add the fruits to the curry sauce.

When the lamb is done, remove from the oven, and let cool. Then cut 4 cups of meat into cubes and mix into the curry sauce. Heat, gently blending all together with up to ½ cup of the wine-flavored cooking juices. Serve on 6 cups of hot fluffy white rice. Yield: about 24 servings.

WATERCRESS AND SAINT BARBARA'S CRESS

We like to make this salad with some of the shining dark green leaves of wild cress. Since they are succulent but slightly bitter, we combine them with such other greens as watercress and lettuces. For this, prepare a simple dressing of bland sesame oil and tarragon vinegar, salt, and freshly-ground pepper.

FESTIVE GREEK BREAD

1 cup milk	3 eggs
1 cup sugar	1 tablespoon lemon juice
½ cup (1 stick) butter	6 cups all-purpose flour, sifted
3 teaspoons salt	1 teaspoon grated nutmeg
2 cakes or packages of yeast	¼ cup sesame seeds
1 cup lukewarm water	1½ cups slivered almonds

Heat the milk to boiling, stir in sugar, butter, and salt. Let mixture cool to lukewarm. Dissolve yeast in the warm water, then stir into the milk-and-sugar mixture. Beat eggs and add. Stir in lemon juice. Sift flour and nutmeg together, then add a cup at a time to the yeast mixture. Add sesame seeds and almonds. Turn out on a floured board and knead for several minutes. Put dough into a greased bowl, cover with waxed paper and refrigerate for 3 hours.

Shape dough into four rings, about 7 inches in diameter, or into twists or braids. Place on greased baking sheets. Let rise in a warm place covered with a towel until doubled in bulk. Then bake for about 20 minutes in a 375-degree oven, or until tester comes out clean. While bread is still warm, spread with Almond-Sugar Frosting. Each ring expands to 8 or 9 inches and will serve 10 to 12 people.

Almond-Sugar Frosting: Mix 3 cups of confectioner's sugar to spreading consistency with 8 to 9 teaspoons of milk and ¼ teaspoon almond extract. Or use rum or sherry in place of milk.

Barbara, the Saint, was elected of God,
She gave her bread to the poor.
Her miserly father rebuked her
And threatened her with his sword.
When he caught her with the bread in her lap
She cried unto God in her fear.
God turned the sword in his hand
Into a crochet needle.
When her father demanded to see
What she concealed in her lap,
She cried unto God for help
And the bread in her lap turned to roses.

—Translation from the Syrian

6
Saint Nicholas's Day—
December 6

At Caprilands the second week of Christmas begins with a colorful festival on December sixth in honor of Saint Nicholas, a favorite saint in many lands. In the nineteenth century, there were more
churches named for him than for any other saint in the calendar.
Unlike the legendary Saint Barbara, Nicholas was an actual person, born in the fourth century in Lycia in Asia Minor to Christian
parents of wealth and position. As a child, he was exceedingly religious; at an early age he became a priest and then a bishop. His
parents died soon after his ordination, leaving him a vast fortune.

He spent this mainly in charity, often making secret gifts to those in need. Today, it is as a giver-of-gifts that Saint Nicholas is remembered. He died on December sixth and was buried in his own cathedral. For centuries his tomb was a shrine. When the city of Myra fell into the hands of the Saracens in 1087, his relics were removed to the Italian seaport of Bari.

Nicholas always appears as a kind-hearted bishop, a protector of children, young girls, schoolboys, and orphans, of the poor, weak, or captive. He is the patron saint of sailors, laborers, merchants who trade by water, and pawnbrokers—the saint of common people and emperors as well.

In one famous story, Nicholas saved the three daughters of an impoverished nobleman. Unable to support them at home or to provide doweries, the father decided to sell his daughters into slavery. Hearing of this, Nicholas rode to their castle and tossed a bag of gold through an open window. When the maidens rushed to see their benefactor, they heard only the sound of distant hoofs. On successive nights two more bags of gold were delivered the same way. Thus equipped with proper doweries, the girls were able to marry, and of course, lived happily ever after.

Eventually, the father discovered his benefactor, and Nicholas became known as the gift-giver. Since that time presents have been given on his day in many lands. And the three bags, rounded out by the coins they contained, are supposed to be the origin of the pawnbrokers' three golden balls that hang outside their shops.

In another tale, Nicholas came to the rescue of a storm-tossed ship. He calmed the waters and helped the sailors bring their ship safely to port. For centuries, sailors have considered Nicholas their patron saint and countless seaport churches have been dedicated to him.

Then there is the account of how Nicholas rescued starving people at a time of famine in Myra. Learning that a grain ship was

SAINT NICHOLAS

in port, he asked that it be partly unloaded. At first the sailors refused, since the cargo had been weighed at Alexandria and full measure was to be delivered to the emperor. But the Bishop promised that their cargo would not be diminished, and the sailors unloaded some of the grain. When they arrived at Alexandria, the weight was indeed the same.

In another famine three schoolboys came to an inn but the innkeeper, having no meat for his customers, cut up the boys and tossed them into a pickling tub. Providently, Nicholas also came to the inn and discovered the bodies in the brine. He blessed them and miraculously the boys came back to life. Thus he became the patron saint of children.

In stained glass, paintings, and prints, Saint Nicholas appears in bishop's robes with a miter, an ornamented cope, and jeweled gloves, holding in his hand a crozier, the staff of his office. Usually he is shown with a long beard, but sometimes he is beardless, an allusion to the youthful age at which he became a bishop. A ship or anchor may accompany him, also the three boys in a tub.

Saint Nicholas, Father Christmas, and Santa Claus

It is not clear just when Saint Nicholas became associated with the pre-Christian, Father Christmas, a beloved personification of the season from the Middle Ages on. There was no connection between him and the Bishop until Teutonic customs crossed the North Sea in the nineteenth century. Then Father Christmas acquired some of the Saint's characteristics. Sailors' devotion to their patron no doubt brought Nicholas to Holland, and when the Dutch settlers came to New Amsterdam (New York), Saint Nicholas or *Sinter Claes* became Santa Claus.

Present-day customs vary from country to country. In Europe, Saint Nicholas, as bearer-of-gifts, wears his bishop's robes and is accompanied by a servant. In Holland, the Saint rides a horse, and on the eve of his festival, Dutch children put out their wooden shoes filled with hay and sugar for his horse. In the morning, they find their shoes filled with chocolates and perhaps shiny coins. Black Peter, the Moorish servant, carries a switch to beat the naughty ones, and so children are always good the weeks before Saint Nicholas comes.

In England and America the ecclesiastic is now part kindly bishop, part mischievous elf. Santa Claus wears a scarlet suit not vestments and drives a reindeer sleigh instead of riding a horse. From a tall ascetic churchman, Saint Nicholas has become a jolly fat burgher with a pack of gifts on his back instead of bags of gold on his saddle. In the Norse tradition, he pops down the chimney to deliver his gifts and drink up potions and porridge left for him as for the dwarfs and trolls. As a Christmas character, Santa Claus combines goodness and generosity, cheer and wisdom—but he is not above a prank or two.

Decorations for Saint Nicholas's Day

At Caprilands, we follow the Dutch story of Saint Nicholas and his bags of gold. Our harvest decorations for Saint Barbara give way to a burst of golden color; our green tubbed trees are now trimmed with tinsel and glittering balls, and gilded holly leaves are tucked into the green ivy wreath around the punch bowl.

Although shining gold is all around us, our symbol for the day is a simple wooden shoe, a sabot brought long ago from Holland. Instead of straw for the Bishop's horse, we place in it an arrangement of broom for Black Peter's switches; mugwort, the herb for foot-sore travelers who trudged behind the Saint; teasel for the cloth merchants whose goods Saint Nicholas protected on long sea voyages, and yellow tansy and yarrow to represent the bags of gold.

Recipes for the Feast of Saint Nicholas

To honor the patron saint of sailors, our recipes emphasize food from the sea, dishes seasoned with spices made popular by Dutch sea captains, and chocolate, always a favorite of the Dutch.

GOLDEN BISHOP PUNCH

2 quarts apricot juice	1 pint apricot brandy
8 sprigs fresh rosemary	1 pint unflavored brandy
1 gallon dry sauterne	Nutmeg
1 quart dry vermouth	Rosemary for garnish

Refrigerate apricot juice with rosemary sprigs for three hours. Combine the wines and brandies. Place a large cake of ice in a punch bowl and pour in the liquids. Grate fresh nutmeg over the top and garnish with fresh rosemary. 8 quarts or approximately 30 servings.

SAINT NICHOLAS RED FRUIT PUNCH WITH SHERBET

This is for children's parties on Saint Nicholas's Day.

1 gallon sweet cider	Sugar (optional)
1 gallon cranberry juice	2 quarts lime sherbet
1 quart orange juice	Long rosemary sprigs
3 quarts mixed fresh fruit (bought in jars)	

Combine the cider and juices with the fruits and check for sweetness. Cranberry may seem tart to some children. Add sugar if necessary. Pour over a cake of ice in a punch bowl, spoon in hardfrozen sherbet, garnish with fresh rosemary, and serve at once. Provide each punch cup with a spoon for eating the fruit and sherbet. Serves 30.

GINGER PICKS

For a spicy, festive-appearing appetizer, alternate small pieces of candied ginger, canned pear, and ham on cocktail picks. Marinate 1 hour in port wine. Drain well and sprinkle with freshly-grated nutmeg before serving.

TUNA SPREAD WITH HERBS

1 13-ounce can water-packed white tuna
2 hard-cooked eggs, chopped fine
¼ cup finely chopped mixed herbs, tarragon, parsley, chives, dill
¼ cup finely-chopped stuffed olives
2 teaspoons lemon juice
Salt
Freshly-ground pepper
2 tablespoons butter
4 tablespoons mayonnaise

Drain tuna and combine with the chopped eggs. Make the herb mixture of a little dried tarragon and a little dill, more of fresh parsley and chives. Combine with tuna and stir in the rest of the ingredients. Serve on crackers. Enough for 12 guests.

SHRIMP-AND-MUSHROOM CASSEROLE WITH DILL

To simplify preparation, buy cleaned frozen shrimp.

1 teaspoon dried tarragon leaves
1 bay leaf
1 teaspoon salt
1 teaspoon whole allspice
1 teaspoon powdered ginger
1 teaspoon caraway seeds
6 whole cloves
2 pounds cleaned frozen shrimp
1 pound fresh mushrooms
¼ pound (1 stick) butter
1 teaspoon powdered (freeze-dry) shallots
¼ cup chopped parsley
2 tablespoons chopped dill weed
2 10½-ounce cans cream-of-chicken soup
4 cups cooked rice

Bring 2 quarts of water to a boil; add tarragon, bay leaf, salt and spices, and simmer a few minutes; then bring to a boil. Add shrimp, cover, and bring again to a boil. Remove from heat and let stand 5 minutes—no longer. Drain. Turn shrimp into a serving casserole. Trim mushrooms, slice, and sauté in butter with shallots. Mix in chopped parsley, dill, and chicken soup. Heat but do not boil. Pour over shrimp in casserole. To serve, spoon shrimp over cooked rice. Makes 15 servings.

CHOCOLATE BREAD

A delectable bread, as rich as cake, to be served for tea.

3 squares unsweetened chocolate
¼ cup butter
¾ cup sugar
1-inch piece vanilla bean grated, *or*
   1 teaspoon vanilla extract
1 egg, beaten

2 cups milk
3½ cups flour
5 teaspoons baking powder
1 teaspoon salt
1 cup walnuts broken into bits
¼ cup sesame seeds

In the top of a double boiler, melt chocolate and butter; stir in sugar and the vanilla bean if using. Combine egg and milk and add to the chocolate mixture. Sift together the flour, baking powder, and salt, and stir this into the chocolate mixture. Beat until smooth. Add walnuts and sesame seeds and vanilla extract if substituting this for the grated vanilla bean. Line two loaf pans with buttered wax paper. Divide dough and turn into the pans. Bake in a preheated 300-degree oven for 1 hour or until tester comes out clean. Cool for 10 minutes, then turn loaves out on a wire rack, remove wax paper, and frost.

Rum Frosting: Mix 2 cups confectioner's sugar with 3½ tablespoons rum. Spread over loaves and decorate with chocolate shot and candied cherry halves.

SPRINGERLES

Springerle, which means lively little horse, is the traditional cooky for Saint Nicholas's Day. These cookies once required the efforts of a whole family since the dough must be beaten for one hour. Today's mechanized mixers make it easier. Quaint wooden molds of birds, animals, flowers, and people stamp designs on the rolled-out dough or you can use an imprinted rolling pin to make the designs. One ingredient, hartshorn, was originally scraped from the horns of the male deer. Today ammonium carbonate is used, and is available from drugstores or baker's supply houses.

3 eggs
1½ cups flour
1½ cups confectioner's sugar
½ teaspoon hartshorn (ammonium
   carbonate) *or* 1 teaspoon baking
   soda

½ teaspoon salt
1 lemon, juice and grated rind
1 tablespoon anise seed

Beat eggs until foamy. Sift flour three times, sift again with sugar, hartshorn or baking soda, and salt. Combine with eggs and beat for 1 hour. Add lemon juice and rind, and anise seed, and beat again to mix thoroughly. Roll out dough on a floured board to ¼-inch thickness. Press molds or carved rolling pin firmly into the dough. Cut into squares and remove with a spatula to a large firm cooky sheet or board to dry for 24 hours. Then preheat oven to 300 degrees. Transfer springerles to a greased cooky sheet and bake for about 20 minutes. Do not let them brown; lower part of cooky turns yellow, top remains white. Makes 25 squares.

Oh day of gold and giving,
Of food for souls and food for living,
Of tales of miracles and might,
Saint Nicholas, keep us in thy sight.—A.G.S.

SAINT LUCY

7
Saint Lucy's Day—December 13

The people of Sweden on December thirteenth joyously welcome Saint Lucy, who brings sight to the blind, food to the hungry, and light in the midst of winter darkness. The Festival of Lights, sometimes called Little Christmas, is the favorite Swedish Advent celebration. In many ways it resembles the pagan rites of the Winter Solstice. However, Saint Lucy belongs to Christian tradition, and she was apparently a real person.

Lucy or Lucia was born to wealthy Christians in Syracuse in Sicily in the third century. While still a child, she secretly vowed to remain a virgin and to dedicate her life and fortune to the Church. Her father died while she was young, so it was her mother who arranged a marriage with a young pagan. Lucia refused him and her rejected suitor denounced her as a Christian to the governor, this in the time of the Diocletian persecutions. Miracles preserved her from a brothel and death by burning, but finally she was martyred by a sword thrust through her neck.

In one legend, to escape the marriage, Lucy tears out her eyes, but they are miraculously restored and she becomes more beautiful than ever. Another story has her blinded by the governor's orders, and in paintings, she sometimes appears holding a book with her own eyes laid upon it. More pleasantly, she is represented carrying a flame or burning lamp, for her name comes from *lux* meaning light.

In the North, Saint Lucy's Day is a festival of fire and light, with two ceremonies, one in the church, the other in the home. In the early morning darkness of December thirteenth, the Lucia Queen or Lucia Bride—usually the youngest child in the family— is dressed in a long white gown, perhaps ornamented with glittering stars. She wears a bilberry (whortleberry) crown fitted with lighted candles as she goes from room to room to awaken family and guests. She brings hot coffee and buns made in the shape of braids, twists, sometimes cats, called *Lucia Kattoir*. These are golden with saffron or flavored with cardamon. Next she visits the barns with a tray of coffee and food for the farmhands; then extra rations are given to all the animals.

In the church ceremony, Lucia is similarly attired. She enters the shadowy church wearing her lighted crown, often accompanied by "star-boys," dressed in blue with peaked caps decorated with stars. They carry star-topped staffs, like the star-boys who make the rounds on Epiphany.

In both ceremonies, Lucia brings light into darkness, fire against winter cold, and promise of sun and new life in spring.

Decorations for the Festival of Lights

At Caprilands we celebrate a whole week of Lucia Days. Our golden decorations for Saint Nicholas are freshened and polished, and a supply of candles laid in for the many evening parties now lighted only by tapers and the hearth fire. Artemisia wreaths with tansy, yarrow, and strawflowers decorate the entrances, and swags of silver artemisia, tinkling with bells, festoon the hallway and the doors to the kitchen. A gilded kissing ball of holly and ivy with sprigs of fragrant rosemary and other herbs is suspended over one doorway, with pieces of pearly mistletoe, the plant that must never touch the ground. To Druids, it was the "all-heal," the soul of their Sacred Oak, not to be defiled by contact with earth.

From the ceiling we hang treasures of Swedish craftsmanship— birds of blond wood, painted blue with specks of gold or vermilion, little straw figures and stars—all suspended on cords to twirl in the warmth and glow of candles. On the mantel we set bright crowing cocks and Lucia's golden cat, for the Saint was of such virtue that she subdued the devil, who entered homes in the guise of a cat. Usually he is curled submissively at her feet. The birds, known as chipcuckoos or Christmas pigeons, appear in legends of Valhalla, their responsibility to awaken the gods before the coming of twilight. As Christian symbols, they represent the Holy Spirit hovering over the home and blessing it.

Dancing trolls, straw figures—including the traditional goat, birds, and animals of gingerbread, Nisse and Nasse—the symbolic bridal couple—cat-shaped saffron buns, and coffee-breads topped with cherries and angelica decorate our tables. For centerpieces, we like braided breads encircling fat candles or tiny baskets filled with yellow tansy, yarrow, and rue. Little wreaths of true myrtle are hung from the candelabra.

Recipes for the Lucia Days

In this week before Christmas steaming glögg scents the kitchen and sends a spicy aroma through the farmhouse. We prepare the warming potion in various ways. This glögg is fairly sweet; we serve it in the afternoon with Christmas cookies rather than before a meal.

CAPRILANDS SPICED JULGLÖGG

2 quarts tawny port
½ cup raisins
½ cup whole blanched almonds
8 cardamon seeds, shelled
10 cloves
4 cinnamon sticks
4 pieces dried ginger root

1 orange, sliced
1 quart brandy
1 cup sugar lumps
1 tablespoon 190-proof alcohol, warmed (optional)
Cinnamon sticks for stirrers

Slowly heat 1 quart of the port with raisins, almonds, seeds, spices, and orange slices. Simmer until steaming. Heat the remaining quart of port until warm (but not steaming) and combine with the spiced portion in serving bowl or copper kettle. Heat brandy separately. Place sugar lumps in a sieve or rack over the bowl, pour hot brandy over the sugar, which melts and drips down. Remove the rack, and sprinkle the warmed alcohol on top of the glögg. Light a match to it; then carry in flaming splendor to the table. Serve in 6-ounce mugs, with the cinnamon sticks, and ladle a few raisins and almonds into each mug. Makes about 16 servings.

HERRING SALAD WITH DILL

This salad and the one that follows are good dishes for a smörgåsbord. Dill is a Swedish favorite lavishly used for this feast day.

2 12-ounce jars herring pickled in
  wine
½ cup dill vinegar
1 teaspoon salt
1 teaspoon freshly-ground pepper
¼ cup coriander seeds
6 firm red apples, sliced not peeled

2 red onions, peeled and sliced
½ cup sweet relish
12 sweet gherkins, sliced
1 tablespoon chopped dill weed
¼ cup chopped parsley
½ cup sour cream
Lettuce

Cut herring into small pieces. Combine vinegar, salt, pepper, and coriander, and pour over the herring. Refrigerate for several hours. Then drain and combine with the apples, onions, relish, and gherkins. Mix chopped dill and parsley with sour cream. Arrange lettuce in a salad bowl and heap herring on it. Top with the sour cream dressing. Makes 25 generous servings.

GREEN BEAN SALAD
(bohenkraut)

4 pounds canned French-style
  green beans
2 pounds canned sliced beets
¼ pound salami
3 onions, chopped
½ cup chopped parsley
1 tablespoon dried summer savory
¼ cup chopped chives

2 cups sweet relish
6 small garlic dill pickles, sliced
1 teaspoon salt
½ teaspoon freshly-ground pepper
1 cup dill vinegar
1 head lettuce
Chopped dill

Rinse beans under cold water and drain well. Drain beets. Cut salami into small pieces, mix with the beans and beets, and the onions, herbs, relish, pickles, and seasonings. Pour herb vinegar over all and chill well. At serving time, drain, and arrange mixture on lettuce. Garnish with chopped dill. Serves about 25.

CREAMED CODFISH WITH DILL

Ling or *lutfisk* is usually served at the Swedish Little Christmas Feast. New England codfish is a good substitute.

1 pound dried salt cod
7 tablespoons butter
1 tablespoon flour
2 cups heavy cream
1 cup light cream
Freshly-ground pepper

8 medium-sized potatoes
1 tablespoon chopped dill weed
¼ cup chopped parsley
3 sliced hard-cooked eggs (op-
    tional)

Put the salt cod in cold water, bring to a boil and simmer 1 hour, changing water twice to remove some of the salt. Rinse under cold water and drain well. Flake the fish. Melt 4 tablespoons of the butter, stir in the flour, then the heavy and light cream and a little pepper. Pour over the fish. Peel potatoes and cook in a separate pan until tender; drain, slice, and arrange in a serving casserole. Sauté dill weed in the 3 tablespoons of butter, add 1 tablespoon of parsley, and pour over the potatoes. Pour in the creamed codfish and sprinkle remaining parsley on top. Garnish with slices of hard-cooked eggs, if you wish. Makes 8 to 10 servings.

LUCIA SAFFRON BREAD

These golden loaves are served at both Christmas and Easter. This is one of Caprilands most popular recipes.

2 packages dry yeast
¼ cup lukewarm water
, 4 tablespoons butter, softened
2 eggs, lightly beaten
2 tablespoons sugar
1 teaspoon salt

1 scant teaspoon saffron threads
1 cup boiling water
1 cup milk, scalded
½ cup chopped almonds
1 cup currants
5 cups sifted all-purpose flour
    (about)

Dissolve yeast in ¼ cup warm water. In a large bowl, mix the butter with the eggs, sugar, and salt. Soak saffron threads in the boiling water for 10 minutes. Stir milk into the butter-and-egg mixture. Add almonds and currants. Let mixture cool to lukewarm; then add yeast. Stir in cooled saffron water. Gradually mix in sifted flour, beating well until smooth.

Place dough on a lightly-floured board and knead vigorously until smooth and satiny. Shape into a ball and place in a greased bowl. Brush top of dough with a little oil or soft butter to prevent drying. Cover bowl with a towel and set in a warm place, about 80 degrees, to rise until doubled in bulk, about 1½ to 2 hours. Punch down dough, divide into three loaves, and place in loaf pans lined with buttered wax paper; let rise again for about 1 hour, or until doubled in bulk. Set pans in a preheated 350-degree oven, and bake about 30 minutes or until food pick comes out clean. When bread is baked, remove from oven and place pans on a rack for about 10 minutes. Then turn the three loaves out of the pans onto a rack to cool.

For the Lucia Festival, we ice the loaves with a frosting of almond-flavored confectioner's sugar, and decorate with yellow raisins in a sunburst design.

CAPRILANDS APPLECAKE, SWEDISH STYLE

In the fall we make applesauce with fine red McIntosh apples, cored, sliced, but cooked with the skin to give the sauce a rosy tint. To 4 cups of sliced apples, add 1 tablespoon of caraway seeds (for a honey flavor) and 1 cup of sugar. Simmer gently, covered, for about 20 minutes. Then purée and leave the skins in the sauce.

Applecake

8 tablespoons (1 stick) butter
5 cups (2 6-ounce packages) zwieback crumbs, crushed
3 cups homemade applesauce

Melt the butter in a skillet, add crumbs and stir until lightly browned. Butter a 2-quart baking dish, and line with crumbs. Alternate layers of applesauce and crumbs, ending with crumbs on top. Bake in a 350-degree oven, uncovered, about 35 to 40 minutes. Cool well, then unmold on a serving plate. Makes 12 large servings.

You can bake the cake the day before the party. The traditional topping is vanilla sauce, but vanilla ice cream or whipped cream will do.

Vanilla Sauce

6 egg yolks, beaten
5 tablespoons sugar
½ vanilla bean, *or* 4 teaspoons
  vanilla extract

2 cups cream, heated
2 cups heavy cream, whipped

To prevent curdling, make this sauce in the top of a double boiler over *simmering water*. Pour egg yolks in the pan and beat in sugar; if using vanilla bean, add now, the bean opened to let seeds flavor the sauce. Stir in warm cream, cook until mixture thickens; keep stirring. Remove from heat; add vanilla extract here if using instead of the bean. Stir occasionally while cooling. Remove vanilla bean and when mixture is cold, fold in whipped cream.

> *Lo, on our thresholds there*
> *White clad, with flame-crowned hair*
> *Santa Lucia, Santa Lucia.*—Traditional song

SAINT FRANCIS

8
Christmas Reveillon—
December 25

Our celebration of Christmas Eve begins when friends gather at Caprilands after the midnight service. In some countries, it is traditional to fast on Christmas Eve—only a light fish soup in Scandinavia, stewed eels in Italy, in Denmark a creamy rice pudding. But after midnight, there is a great feast! The French call the occasion *Reveillon* and preparations occupy most of December twenty-fourth. Since we return from church in the early morning hours, cold and hungry, everything must be ready. A happy confusion fills our kitchen as guests warm themselves by the old iron cookstove and enjoy a first round of Caprilands Christmas daiquiris. Then we move our merry company to the living room. The yule log crackles, candlelight shines on the dark chestnut beams, the pomanders twinkle as they spin on long cords, and the warm air is fragrant with spices and rosemary. Our brimming punch bowl placed in the Ivy-and-Holly Wreath is accompanied by little earthenware crocks with spreads for crackers or breads. Salads and a casserole are served as hors d'oeuvres. In this way, with carols and laughter, our joyful Christmas Day begins.

Decorations for Reveillon

On Christmas Eve each corner of the keeping room glows with a decorated tree; bells tinkle sweetly in the dark narrow hall. Great glossy-leaved branches of holly, heavy with red berries, are arranged in handsome vermilion pots to decorate the serving table and mantel. Saint Nicholas's shoe, Lucia's cat, mistletoe on the old flax wheel, and small nativity scenes in new greens on the bookshelves bring together the festivals of the long Christmas. Big pots of bay now join those of rosemary, and the crèche holds fresh manger herbs. The fragrance of burning frankincense and myrrh mingles with woodsmoke and the appetizing kitchen odors of the Reveillon Feast.

Recipes for Reveillon

DAIQUIRI BOWL

We serve our favorite Christmas punch in a white Italian pottery bowl decoratively wreathed in a raised design of green holly leaves. The bowl rests on a circle of growing ivy and berried holly. Tall rosemary plants on a bench behind the table complete a festive setting.

2¼ cups (12 lemons) lemon juice
2¼ cups (12 limes) lime juice
1 pint water
2 cups sugar (about)

3 quarts white Bacardi-type rum
1 cup cranberry juice (optional)
2 limes, sliced
Maraschino cherries

Combine lemon and lime juice with water and add sugar to taste. Refrigerate several hours. Place in blender with one tray of ice cubes and blend until foamy. At serving time, put two trays of ice cubes in a punch bowl, add the juice mixture, and pour in the rum. Color the punch with cranberry juice, if you wish, and garnish with lime slices and cherries. The melting ice dilutes the alcohol. Serves 12 very generously.

LOBSTER SPREAD

2 cups finely-chopped cooked lobster
2 tablespoons olive oil
3 shallots, finely chopped, *or* 1 tablespoon powdered freeze-dry shallots
½ cup dry white wine

1 tablespoon hot prepared herb mustard
3 tablespoons chopped parsley
2 tablespoons grated Parmesan cheese
1 8-ounce package cream cheese

Sauté lobster gently in oil with shallots. Add white wine and simmer until wine is reduced to about 2 tablespoons. Remove from heat, stir in mustard, parsley, and grated cheese. Then whip in the cream cheese. Pack in earthenware crocks and store in refrigerator. Makes 2½ cups. Serves 12.

HOLIDAY SALAD

This is both relish and salad. Sweet and sour, hot and bland, chewy and delightful, the ingredients alone will fill a shopping cart. This large recipe can be used on a number of occasions during the holidays.

1 16-ounce can whole corn, drained
1 16-ounce can chick peas, drained
1 16-ounce can kidney beans, drained
1 4-ounce jar Vienna sausages, sliced
1 15-ounce package raisins
1 cup chopped dates
1 cup chopped almonds
2 sweet Italian onions, chopped
1 12-ounce jar hot piccalilli
1 pint spring salad (comes in glass jar)

1 pint sweet relish
1 3-ounce jar sweet pickled onions
1 8-ounce jar sour onions
1 12-ounce jar hot pepper relish
2 cups brown sugar
1 4-ounce jar prepared hot herb mustard
2 cloves garlic, crushed
2 tablespoons chili powder
1 cup chopped fresh parsley, *or* ½ cup dried parsley
1 teaspoon dried summer savory

Just mix all the ingredients together and put in jars. Cover and store in the refrigerator. Serve well-chilled on a bed of lettuce or chicory. Makes about 12 pounds.

ROAST GOOSE

If you are preparing this feast for your return from midnight service, put the stuffed goose in a 325-degree oven about nine o'clock and baste frequently until you leave for church. Let roasting continue, and on your return, by one or one-thirty a.m., the goose will be ready. It can wait 30 to 40 minutes in a hot turned-off oven if the door is left ajar.

Stuffing for a 12-pound goose

1 cup chopped onions
Goose liver, finely chopped
½ cup (1 stick) butter
4 cups breadcrumbs
4 cups peeled chopped apples
1 cup raisins
1½ teaspoons salt
½ teaspoon pepper

½ teaspoon ground mace
½ teaspoon freshly-grated nutmeg
2 tablespoons Caprilands Poultry Seasoning (see note below)
¼ cup chopped parsley
Lemon juice
Salt

Sauté onions and liver in butter for several minutes; add bread-crumbs and brown. Stir in apples and raisins, and add seasonings and parsley. Toss all together lightly.

Rub the goose inside and out with lemon juice and salt. Remove any loose heavy fat. Stuff and secure with skewers or sew up cavity. Prick skin all over with a fork to let fat out during cooking. Place the goose on a rack in a roasting pan.

Prepare a basting liquid of 1 cup dry white wine, juice of 1 lemon, ¼ cup rosemary, and about 1 tablespoon salt. Pour some of this over the goose and cover it with leaves of an herb called beifuss (*Artemisia vulgaris*) if you have it. (This is an old German custom; beifuss leaves and buds were also added to the stuffing.) Otherwise cover lightly with foil.

Roast in a preheated 325-degree oven, basting frequently (until time for church) and drain fat from pan at least twice. After 2½ hours, remove foil if using it. A 12-pound goose takes about 4 hours. It is done when legs pull easily from the body and juices run pale yellow when fleshiest part of drumstick is pricked. (*Note:* Caprilands Poultry Seasoning has a parsley base with sage, rosemary, thyme, marjoram, onion, ginger, nutmeg, and salt.)

CRANBERRY RELISH MOLD

To accompany the Christmas goose, this colorful red salad can be made in a star or Christmas-tree mold.

1 pound fresh cranberries
1 cup sugar
1 cup water
1 8-ounce package cream cheese
1½ cups cottage cheese
Salt

1 cup prepared horseradish
2 envelopes unflavored gelatin, softened in ½ cup cold water
Rosemary sprays
Extra horseradish for garnish

Wash and pick over cranberries. Boil sugar and water together about 5 minutes. Then add cranberries and cook gently, keeping as many cranberries whole as possible. Set aside enough whole cranberries to outline the mold. Mix remaining cranberries with cream cheese, cottage cheese, a pinch of salt and the cup of horseradish. Stir softened gelatin into the cheese-and-horseradish mixture. Turn into a 2-quart mold, brushed with cooking oil, and chill. To serve, unmold on sprays of rosemary and decorate the outline with the saved whole cranberries and extra horseradish. Serves 12.

TRIPLE-SEED HOLIDAY CAKE

3 cups sifted all-purpose flour
2½ teaspoons baking powder
¾ teaspoon grated nutmeg
1 teaspoon salt
⅔ cup Crisco or other shortening
2 cups sugar
4 eggs, unbeaten

3 tablespoons grated lemon rind
1 cup milk
1 tablespoon caraway seeds
1 tablespoon poppy seeds
1 teaspoon anise seeds
Powdered sugar

Sift together the flour, baking powder, nutmeg, and salt. In a separate bowl, cream together shortening and sugar; add 1 egg at a time, beating about 1 minute after each addition. Blend in lemon rind. Gradually add flour mixture to the shortening and eggs, alternating flour with small amounts of milk, stirring and mixing well.

Grease and flour a tube pan and spread one-quarter of the batter on the bottom. Sprinkle with caraway seeds. Pour in another quarter of the batter and sprinkle with poppy seeds. Add the third quarter and sprinkle with anise seeds. Then top with remaining batter.

Bake in a preheated 350-degree oven for about 80 minutes. Remove from the oven, but let cool on a rack for 15 minutes before removing cake from the pan. Sprinkle with powdered sugar or frost if you prefer.

LEGENDS OF THE CRÈCHE
AND THE MANGER HERBS

The Crèche of Saint Francis of Assisi

The first crèche was probably set up by Saint Francis in his hermitage at Greccio, a town situated high on a rock above a dark forest. In a grotto, Saint Francis arranged a representation of the Holy Family with a little crib made by the monks. A great white ox stood on one side, a gentle little donkey on the other. At an altar above the crib, the midnight Eucharist was celebrated, and the frosty breath of the animals rose like incense. The peasants trudged up the hillside to worship, young and old gathering around the grotto to await the miracle of the holy birth. After the mass, Saint Francis stretched out his arms to the crib as though the Holy Child were actually there, and the intensity of his belief filled the empty manger with the radiance of the Christ.

From this first simple crèche of Greccio the custom of representing the scene at Bethlehem has spread throughout the Christian world. The crèche became a means of teaching, and from it was developed the miracle play. Before a homemade crèche, children, like those of old Provence, have said this prayer since earliest times.

> *Little Jesus of the crib*
> *Give us the virtues of those that surround you*
> *Make us philosophical as the fishermen*
> *Carefree as the drummer*
> *Merry, in exploring the world as the troubadour*
> *Eager for work as the bugler*
> *Patient as the spinner*
> *Kind as the ass*
> *Strong as the ox that keeps you warm.*—Traditional

Animals of the stable

These are represented as possessing attributes of man. The horse resented having his good food used for bedding, and hungrily ate away the soft hay until the Christ Child lay on the bare boards of the manger. Mary, patiently replacing the hay, remonstrated with the beast and said, "For your selfishness, you will be bound to the service of man forever and you will be hungry no matter how much you eat."

The ox gave his hay willingly and kept the Child warm with the heat of his breath, and so he was blessed. The cow presented her new calf as an offering. Touched by their devotion, Mary promised that these animals should relish their food so much that they would chew it again and again, and the cow would be blessed with a new calf each year.

The mule, whose laugh disturbed the sleep of the Babe, and the noisy goat were punished by Mary, "The mule shall never bear young, and the goat's voice shall be disliked by man forever."

The manger herbs

BASIL was a favorite charm in Greece and used to banish the mysterious beings called Karkanzari, who made peasant life almost unbearable. These mischievous creatures wandered about through the twelve days of Christmas, supposedly they were the souls who had found no rest in heaven and had returned to disturb the living. To banish such trouble, the priest came to each house with a cross adorned with sprigs of basil. He dipped this in holy water, and sprinkled and blessed each room and the environs of the house. Then the Karkanzari disappeared.

BEDSTRAW was one of the plants of Palestine that was cut with hay and fed to animals. Thus it was with the hay in the stable where the Christ Child was born. Bedstraw once blossomed white and scentless, but on the holy night the flowers turned to purest gold and a heavenly fragrance filled every minute blossom. Thus bedstraw became one of the most revered of plants, too sacred for the touch of devils; after the Christmas festivities, it was scattered over the fields to bless and increase the crops. It was also spread in stalls to protect animals from disease, and on Christmas Eve heaped on the floor for the family to sleep upon.

PENNYROYAL in the past was woven into wreaths to be worn on the head as protection against giddiness. Culpeper wrote, "Drink it with wine, it is good for venomous bites, and applied to the nostrils with vinegar revives those who faint and swoon."

ROSEMARY, often blossoming at Christmas, a mist of tiny flowers like dewdrops on the rich green branches, is called dew-of-the-sea, sometimes Romero, or the Pilgrim's flower. In Spain and Italy, it was considered a charm against witches; in England and on the Continent, after being dipped in scented water, it was used in the bride's wreath, and also presented to the wedding guests as a symbol of love and loyalty. Sometimes bunches were richly gilded and tied with colored ribbons.

THYME also grew abundantly in Palestine on rocky gravelly soil and was cut with other grasses for the manger. Its antiseptic fragrance kept away vermin and gave the bed a sweet clean smell. A symbol of bravery, thyme is associated with the Holy Child, who would endure much suffering; with Mary, the Lady of Sorrows; with Joseph, who needed great courage and patience.

THE CHRISTMAS ROSE that dares to bloom in the snow earned the name, "Christe Herbe." On the night when the Wise Men, following the star, journeyed toward Bethlehem, a little girl came after them. Struggling to keep up with the excited men, she arrived breathless at the manger. There she saw the kneeling kings presenting their rich gifts of gold, frankincense, and myrrh. Ashamed to be without an offering, she withdrew to the flocks on the hillside, and standing disconsolately among them, prayed for a gift that she might present.

Suddenly, with a rush of wings, a glowing angel stood before her. He waved a wand of lilies over the ground and at once hundreds of white waxen blossoms appeared. The little girl gathered all she could carry and hurried back to the stable with her precious load. When she reached the manger, the Christ Child turned from the gifts of gold and reached out tiny hands to grasp the flowers. Mary placed them in the manger, saying to the little girl, "My child, you are blessed, for this is a gift from the heart, greater than riches, sweeter than rare perfume, a symbol of love."

THE THREE KINGS

9
New Year's Day—
January 1

The Roman kalends of January ushered in the new year with three days of feasting, masquerades, divinations, and gifts to children and the poor. The Church considered January first the date of the circumcision of Christ. After the fourth century this was called Saint Basil's Day, and the day is still observed in Greece, Rumania, and Albania, where a coin concealed in a cake brings prosperity to the lucky one who finds it.

In the Middle Ages, the beginning of the year was celebrated after the spring equinox, on March twenty-fifth, when dark winter gave way to new green and the moon was full. With the shift to the Gregorian calendar in the sixteenth century, many European countries changed New Year's Day back to January first. But not until 1752 did England and Colonial America accept this date for new year festivities.

France still follows the Roman custom of gifts on New Year's Day instead of on Christmas or Saint Lucy's Day or the Eve of Saint Nicholas. In Spain and Italy, presents are appropriately exchanged on Epiphany, the time of the arrival of the gift-bearing Three Kings. In our own country, the new year is always an occasion for celebration, of cheerful noise and many resolutions. Gifts are not generally exchanged, but a handsome feast is customary.

Decorations for New Year's Day

Since many Advent decorations remain, we need only replace the drying holly and add a few touches of glitter. We bring out our glass-prismed candlesticks and cut-glass decanters; we spray holly leaves and cones with gold to place among green boughs and the ivy ring around the punch bowl. On New Year's Day we present each guest with one of the pomanders that decorate our Spice Tree. These are tied with rosemary sprays for remembrance and rue to keep away evil.

Recipes for the New Year Feast

At Caprilands we serve a late afternoon buffet for invited guests, since our country isolation precludes casual callers. On this occasion our punch bowl is a bright copper basin brimming with a frothy mixture of hot spiced ale, brandy, beaten eggs, and roasted apples.

OLDE ENGLISH WASSAIL

This is the time to "Wassail the trees that they may beare you many a plum and many a peare." This involved recipe is prepared only for special guests. It is almost a meal in itself and should be served with spoons.

15 small perfect apples or preferably crabapples	6 coriander seeds
2 cups water	3 cardamon seeds
1 teaspoon grated nutmeg	2 quarts ale
2 teaspoons ground ginger	1 quart sherry
3 sticks cinnamon	2 cups sugar
12 cloves	12 eggs, separated
	1 pint brandy

Core apples or crabapples and bake in a 350-degree oven about 20 minutes or until soft but not broken. Simmer in a saucepan for 10 minutes, water, spices, and 1 quart of ale. Add the second quart of ale, sherry, and sugar. Heat again but do not boil. Beat egg whites until they are stiff. Beat yolks until pale in color. Now *slowly* strain half the hot ale mixture over the egg yolks and pour into a warmed metal bowl. Reheat the ale-and-sherry mixture until steaming, then add to the bowl. Warm the brandy and pour it in. Fold in beaten egg whites and add roasted apples—the "lamb's wool and roasted crabs" of Shakespeare. Place an apple in each mug. Serves 15.

CAPRILANDS WALNUT-CHEESE ROLLS WITH HERBS

1 package (8-ounce) cream cheese	⅛ teaspoon dried rosemary
½ pound processed cheddar cheese	⅛ teaspoon dried thyme
4 tablespoons dry sherry	Salt
½ cup finely-ground walnuts	Freshly-ground pepper
1 teaspoon grated onion	4 or more tablespoons chili powder
½ teaspoon garlic powder	

Let cream cheese soften at room temperature; combine with cheddar and sherry. Mash in walnuts, grated onion, and seasonings, except the chili powder. Cut waxed paper into pieces big enough to hold to a roll about 8 inches long, 1½ inches across. Divide cheese mixture into 6 to 8 portions, shape on the waxed paper into rolls, and sprinkle with chili powder, tossing until coated. Place each roll on a section of paper, twist ends together, wrap in foil, and freeze. Keep rolls frozen until ready to use, then slice while still cold (do not spread), and serve on crackers.

CORNED BEEF SPREAD

1 1-pound can corned beef
1 8-ounce package cream cheese
½ cup (1 stick) butter, softened
1 medium onion, grated
2 tablespoons chopped chives
½ teaspoon thyme

½ cup fresh parsley chopped, *or*
  2 tablespoons dried parsley
⅛ teaspoon Worchestershire Sauce
1 teaspoon salt
½ teaspoon pepper
Parsley sprigs

Mash corned beef with cream cheese, butter, onion, herbs, and seasonings. Shape into loaf and chill. Garnish with parsley sprigs. Serves 25.

BAKED HAM WITH APRICOTS

6-pound center-cut or canned bone-
  less smoked ham
1 clove garlic, crushed in garlic
  press
1 4-ounce jar prepared herb mustard

25 whole cloves
1 cup brown sugar
1 1-pound can whole apricots
4 to 6 slices canned pineapple
2 cups dry white wine
Parsley, watercress or endive

Preheat oven to 350 degrees. Place the ham on a piece of heavy aluminum foil large enough to fold over the top. Add crushed garlic to mustard. Insert whole cloves over sides and top of ham; spread on mustard and brown sugar. Place some of the apricots and pineapple slices on top. Pull foil up around the sides of the ham, pour on the wine, then fold foil over the top. Bake for about 2 hours. Serve on a platter decorated with the greens and remaining apricots and pineapple slices. Serves 15.

FESTIVE POTATO SALAD

This is one of our most popular salads. It can be made well ahead, refrigerated, and served piled high in cone shape to look like a Christmas tree decorated with "ornaments" of green pickles and red pimiento and stuffed olives.

9½ cups (about 12) boiled potatoes, cubed
12 hard-cooked eggs, chopped
1 large onion, grated, *or* 1 cup chopped chives
2 cups mayonnaise
2 teaspoons mixed dried herbs
1 teaspoon dill seed

½ cup chopped fresh salad burnet
½ clove garlic, crushed
2 teaspoons tarragon vinegar
1 teaspoon salt
Freshly-ground pepper
1 cup stuffed green olives, chopped
½ cup chopped pimientos
6 dill pickles, chopped

Mix together potatoes, eggs, and onion or chives. In a separate bowl combine mayonnaise with dried herbs, dill seed, salad burnet, garlic, vinegar, salt, and pepper. Pour this dressing over the potatoes. Stir in half the chopped olives, pimientos, and pickles, reserving the rest for garnish. Refrigerate for several hours or longer. Line platter with lettuce, shape salad in a tall cone, and decorate with the rest of the olives, pimientos, and pickles. Serves 15.

ADELMA'S NUTMEG ROLLS

⅓ cup (5⅓ tablespoons) butter
¾ cup sugar
3 eggs, beaten
4 cups flour, sifted
2 teaspoons baking soda
4 teaspoons baking powder

1 teaspoon salt
1½ cups sour cream
1 teaspoon lemon juice
2 teaspoons sesame seeds
1½ cups ground almonds
1 whole nutmeg, grated

Cream butter and sugar. Add eggs and mix well. Sift together flour, baking soda, baking powder, and salt. Stir in sour cream, lemon juice, sesame seeds, almonds, and nutmeg. Combine with sugar-and-egg mixture. Chill for two hours. Drop by spoonfuls onto an ungreased baking sheet, about an inch apart. Bake until golden brown, approximately 15 minutes in a 350-degree oven. Makes about 50. Serve with sweet butter and jam.

HERB-FLAVORED BUTTER COOKIES

These thin, delicately flavored herb cookies, accompanied by fresh fruit or sherbet, are a fitting conclusion to a sumptuous meal.

¼ pound (1 stick) butter	¼ teaspoon salt
1 cup sugar	¼ cup crushed coriander seeds, *or*
1 egg	1 tablespoon whole cumin seeds
1½ cups flour, sifted	Vanilla sugar for decoration
1 teaspoon baking powder	

Cream together butter, sugar, and egg. Sift flour, baking powder and salt together, and mix in coriander or cumin seeds. Stir flour mixture in with butter mixture. Work batter until smooth. Chill overnight. Then on a floured board, roll out dough very thin. Cut with a round 2-inch cutter. Place on a greased cooky sheet, and bake in a 350-degree oven about 10 minutes. If you wish, before baking sprinkle with sugar in which a vanilla bean has been stored for flavor. Makes about 60 cookies.

Happy, happy, New Year
Till next year, till eternity,
Corn on the cornstalk,
Grapes in the vineyard,
Yellow grain in the bin,
Red apples in the garden,
Silkworms in the house,
Happiness and health
Until next year.—Translated from the Bulgarian

10
Epiphany—
January 6

The twelve days of Christmas end with Epiphany, January sixth, when the arrival of the Three Kings in Bethlehem is celebrated. Epiphany means appearance or manifestation, and it is claimed that on this occasion Christ was first revealed as divine to the Gentiles. Balthasar, Caspar, and Melchior, who came from the East, represent the world outside Jewry. Originally January sixth commemorated Christ's baptism. Since the fifth century, it has been the Feast of Epiphany, except in Eastern churches.

In homes and churches where Christmas cribs are set up, the

journey of the Kings is sometimes re-enacted. On Christmas Eve the Kings are still in a remote corner of the room or nave, and on each of the twelve days, guided by the star, they are moved closer to the manger scene. When they finally arrive, they offer their gifts of gold, frankincense, and myrrh. In Spain and Italy, January sixth is still the day when gifts are given.

Twelfth Night or the Eve of Epiphany was originally a pagan celebration. Dating from the Roman Saturnalia when a mock king was chosen from among the slaves to preside over revels, masquerades have been traditional. In the Middle Ages a Lord of Misrule was appointed to direct festivities in the great houses; wild tricks, practical jokes, and upheaval of the social order prevailed. In the sixteenth and seventeenth centuries the Puritans put a stop to much of the carnival but not to certain agricultural rites. In England, orchards were wassailed and fires were lighted to drive off evil spirits. In parts of Europe, masked children led noisy torchlight processions with clanging bells and blowing horns to frighten away the devil.

In a religious vein, boys dressed as the Three Kings sang "star songs" as they strolled through the villages of Austria and southern Germany, led by a fourth boy holding a star-topped pole. One such carol, *A Star Song,* by Robert Herrick begins:

> *Declare to us bright star if we shall seek*
> *Him in the morning's blushing cheek*
> *Or search the bed of spices through*
> *To find him out?*

Decorations for Twelfth Night

Our trees are still fresh-looking and fragrant, and the glittering holly from New Year's decks the ivy ring around the punch bowl and enlivens garlands and mantels. To honor the Wise Men, we renew the herbs in the crèche—thyme, bedstraw, rue, horehound, pennyroyal, and rosemary. Among them we place their gifts— gold in the form of a small cross, aromatic myrrh, and frankincense. Gold stars are the appropriate symbol, and we hang many on threads from the chestnut beams to twinkle in the candlelight. As our guests arrive for the Twelfth-Night Feast, we light candles and burn the pungent resins with spices.

For me it was a great discovery that this wonderful fragrance of haunting memory was available for our Christmas ceremonies. I found that myrrh alone burns with an acrid bitter odor but is most pleasant combined with the sweeter resin of frankincense. As the ancient Egyptians and Hebrews knew, the proportion should be approximately six frankincense to one of myrrh. Burn over low heat. Put an ember from the fire on a hearth shovel and shake the incense sparingly over it, then let it burn on the hearth. Or place ember and incense in a thin pan on the stove over low heat; don't allow it to flame.

Ours is a masquerade party. Costumed guests bring verses to read or carols for all to sing. We provide a traditional wassail or a strong potion known as Fish House Punch. A magnificent crown roast is the great dish and the feast concludes with the traditional Twelfth-Night Cake. Baked in it are a bean and a pea; the man—we always hope it will be a man—who finds the bean in his slice is the Twelfth-Night King and the girl who finds the pea, the Queen.

The most famous Twelfth-Night party is still given at the Drury Lane Theatre in London where a great cake is served to the actors after the performance on January sixth, this festivity in memory of Robert Baddeley, an actor and chef, who left a fund for it.

Recipes for Twelfth Night

CAPRILANDS FISH HOUSE PUNCH

4 cups strong tea
1½ cups sugar (about)
6 cups orange juice
2 cups lemon juice

1 pint peach brandy
12 peach halves
2 quarts dark Jamaica rum
1 quart cognac

Prepare the tea, dissolve sugar in it, and stir in the orange and lemon juice. Refrigerate. Pour peach brandy over the peach halves and refrigerate them also. About 2 hours before serving, place a large chunk of ice in your punch bowl, and pour over it the rum, cognac, and tea and brandy mixtures. Let the punch mellow until serving time. Makes about 7 quarts or serves 25. *Note:* The tea does not taste but helps cut the alcohol and round out the punch. Sample before serving; you may want to add more sugar.

GREEN DEVIL CANAPÉS

2 4½-ounce cans deviled ham
4 tablespoons butter
1 tablespoon herb-flavored prepared mustard
1 8-ounce package cream cheese
1 teaspoon dry mustard
1 teaspoon dried marjoram
¼ cup chopped parsley

¼ cup chopped freeze-dry chives
¼ cup chopped watercress
¼ cup chopped celery leaves
¼ cup chopped spinach leaves
Pinch cayenne pepper
Freshly-ground black pepper
Tabasco sauce

Blend ingredients, mixing well and adding pepper and Tabasco sauce to taste. Spread on toast rounds. Serves 12 amply.

WORTBREAD

This dark richly-flavored bread is made up in large amounts to be stored for use all through the Christmas season. You will need a large bowl for mixing since this recipe makes three to four loaves. Kneading is very important to the texture.

4 packages dry yeast
2 tablespoons sugar
1 cup lukewarm water
1 cup milk, scalded
½ cup hot water
¼ cup Guinness stout
1 cup molasses
½ cup shortening or butter
¼ cup caraway seeds
2 tablespoons salt
4 tablespoons grated orange rind

2 eggs, beaten
4 cups sifted white flour
4 cups sifted whole-wheat flour, *or*
2 cups rye flour combined with
2 cups whole-wheat flour
Extra white flour (approximately
¾ cup for kneading board)
Extra butter for greasing hands
while kneading, 2 tablespoons
melted butter for top of dough

Dissolve yeast and sugar in lukewarm water. In a large bowl, combine hot milk, hot water, stout, molasses, and shortening with caraway seeds, salt, and orange rind. Let cool to lukewarm; then add dissolved yeast and beaten eggs. Sift the 8 cups of flour together. Gradually stir into the yeast mixture. Sprinkle some of the extra flour on a board, turn out dough, grease hands with butter, and knead about 5 minutes, or until dough is smooth. Place in a greased bowl, brush dough with melted butter, cover with waxed paper, and let rise in a warm place for about 2 hours, or until doubled in bulk. Punch the dough down again, let it rest a few minutes, butter hands, and knead again for 5 minutes. Then shape into three or four loaves. Place on greased cooky sheets for round loaves or in greased bread pans for oblong shapes. Cover and let rise again, about 1 hour. Preheat oven to 400 degrees. Bake loaves 10 minutes; reduce heat to 350 degrees and bake for about 30 minutes more, or until a tester comes out clean. Cool on a wire rack, removing from bread pans, if used, after 20 minutes. Store, wrapped in foil, in refrigerator or freezer.

CROWN ROAST OF BEEF

In place of the customary crown roast of pork, we have the butcher shape a 12-pound rib roast of beef into a handsome crown, with paper frills. We roast it in a slow 300-degree oven to keep the beef rare, and occasionally baste with about 2 cups of red wine. Decked with parsley garlands, the roast comes to the table on a platter lined with rosemary sprigs, an extravagant but fitting dish for the Feast of the Three Kings.

CAPRILANDS BEEF PUDDING

We cannot call this Yorkshire Pudding for we have added both seasonings and baking powder, which would distress a Yorkshireman. To have enough drippings for the pudding, we put extra suet in the roasting pan.

6 eggs
3 cups milk
3 cups flour, sifted
1 teaspoon salt
2 teaspoons baking powder

1 teaspoon herb mixture (grind together in a mortar 1 teaspoon each of dried sage, rosemary, parsley, thyme)

Beat eggs until fluffy. Stir in milk. Sift into a bowl, flour, salt, and baking power, then add herb seasoning. Beat in the eggs and milk, and continue beating the batter until well blended. Let stand in a cool place until ready to use. Pour off 1 cup of pan drippings from roast. Heat oven to 450 degrees. Place a baking pan in the oven with ¼ inch of drippings until both are hot. Pour in the batter and over it the remaining pan drippings. Bake in the 450-degree oven for 10 minutes. Reduce heat to 350 degrees and bake 15 to 20 minutes longer. Cut in squares and serve hot with the roast.

TWELFTH-NIGHT CAKE

A splendid combination of fruits and spices, this cake contains the traditional pea and bean to designate the King and Queen for the night's festivities.

How, now the mirth comes
With the cake full of plums,
Where Beam's the King of the sport here;
  Beside we must know,
  The Pea also
Must revell, as Queene, *in the Court here.*—Robert Herrick

½ pound (2 sticks) butter
1 cup brown sugar
4 eggs
¼ cup milk
¼ cup brandy or sherry
1 tablespoon molasses
3½ cups flour, sifted
1 teaspoon baking soda
½ teaspoon ground allspice
1 teaspoon ground cinnamon

¼ cup coriander seeds
1 cup raisins
1 cup currants
½ cup candied cherries
1 cup mixed candied peels
½ cup chopped almonds
1 dried bean, wrapped in foil
1 dried pea, wrapped in foil
Almonds, angelica, cherries, etc.,
  for decoration

Cream butter and sugar together. Add eggs, one at a time, and beat well. Heat together milk, brandy or sherry and molasses, and combine with sugar mixture. In a separate bowl, sift together 3 cups of the flour with soda, spices, and seeds. Then beat into the egg-and-sugar mixture. Sift remaining ½ cup of flour over the fruits, peels, and almonds, and toss to coat lightly. Then add to the batter. When this is thoroughly mixed, fold in the pea and bean. (I wrap them in foil to make them easy to find.)

Preheat oven to 250 degrees. Grease a 2-quart tube pan or line a 9- by 12-inch cake pan with waxed paper, pour in batter, and bake slowly, about 2¼ to 2½ hours. Let cool, then cover with almond-flavored, powdered-sugar frosting and decorate with whole blanched almonds, candied angelica, cherries, and other candied fruits. You may want to make a crown of golden citron pieces and serve the cake on a gold foil mat; in that case, bake in the round tube pan.

LEGEND OF LA BEFANA

Associated with Epiphany is La Befana, her name, Epiphana, contracted to Befana. Represented as a misshapen old woman, she was really not the witch that she resembled but a good fairy searching for the lost Babe of Bethlehem and a friend to all children. In Spain, Italy, and throughout southern Europe, she distributes presents at the Feast of Epiphany.

The broom plant is appropriate for her since she was a busy housekeeper. The broom was doomed to ignominy, forever to sweep the dirt of the earth, because it rustled and snapped so loud that the Roman soldiers almost discovered Mary and the Infant in hiding. And the broom was the plant chosen by witches to ride upon.

So house-proud was Befana that neighbors and passers-by dared not come in for fear of soiling her home. No one knew that she was really good and kind, a lonely soul who had lived too long with her memories. She had been a happy wife and mother but her family had died in a plague many years ago and all that was left to remind her of them was a chest of children's toys.

One night Befana opened her door to three foreigners who asked the way to a town called Bethlehem. They were richly dressed and one wore a crown. They told of a star that would guide them to the place where they might worship a new-born king who would rule the world.

Befana longed to follow them, but housework prevented her. Soon other seekers of the Child came to her door, and each one increased her longing, until she could resist no longer and determined to set forth. Remembering that all the travelers carried gifts for the Child, she selected from among her most cherished possessions a shabby straw doll dressed in a bit of handwoven wool. She also found a great seed pod, round like a ball, something a little boy would like to play with. She added a bundle of herbs for the young mother's health.

But Befana was too late. She had hesitated too long over the small affairs of her household. The shepherds and Wise Men had departed, the star had faded with the dawn, and no one knew where the Christ Child lay. So Befana wanders to this day, and every Twelfth Night she goes from house to house, lifting the bed clothes of sleeping children in her search for the Holy Babe. As she departs, she leaves a little gift in his memory.

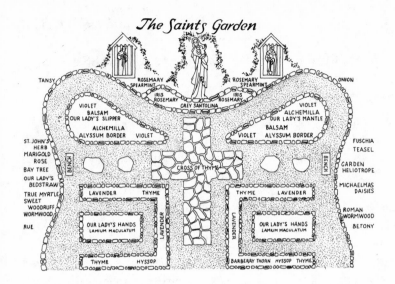

The Saints Garden

TANSY
ROSEMARY SPEARMINT
IRIS ROSEMARY
ROSEMARY SPEARMINT
IRIS ROSEMARY
ONION

VIOLET
BALSAM
OUR LADY'S SLIPPER
ALCHEMILLA
ALYSSUM BORDER   VIOLET
GREY SANTOLINA
VIOLET
ALCHEMILLA
OUR LADY'S MANTLE
BALSAM
VIOLET   ALYSSUM BORDER

ST. JOHN'S HERB
MARIGOLD
ROSE
BAY TREE
OUR LADY'S BEDSTRAW
TRUE MYRTLE
SWEET WOODRUFF
WORMWOOD
RUE

BENCH

CROSS OF THYME

BENCH

FUSCHIA
TEASEL
GARDEN HELIOTROPE
MICHAELMAS DAISIES
ROMAN WORMWOOD
BETONY

LAVENDER   THYME

THYME   LAVENDER

OUR LADY'S HANDS
LAMIUM MACULATUM

LAVENDER

LAVENDER

OUR LADY'S HANDS
LAMIUM MACULATUM

THYME   HYSSOP

BARBERRY THORN HYSSOP THYME

11
Growing the Christmas Garden

With Christmas gifts and decorations in mind, we now consider
how to grow and harvest a number of particularly versatile herbs.
Each herb selected has more than one use: for the wreaths and
trees described in earlier sections of this book; for sachets and
pomanders, delicious jellies, teas, vinegars, and seasonings—the
gift suggestions of the next chapter. Any of these will bring
pleasure to those who share with you a love of herbs.

CULTURE OF THIRTY-SIX HERBS

Ambrosia, *Chenopodium botrys*

A charming, fragrant annual that usually appears in the New England garden in May, sometimes not till June. Seedlings look like little oak trees, hence the early name Jerusalem-oak. Leaves are olive-green and deeply cut, like those of an oak, and purple-red beneath.

If you can locate it, sow the seed yourself. Plants, carefully lifted with a fair amount of soil, can be transplanted, but seldom do self-sown seedlings attain full height and beauty, although they make a good stand for the next year. Watch out for a medicinal weed of the same family that comes up with the true seedlings; it is easy when weeding to pull up the desirable plants. On this account, ambrosia has become quite rare.

It grows rapidly out of a tiny tap root, and from a crown, a lime-green plume shoots up to three feet. The temptation is to pick it to include in early summer bouquets, since it smells sweet and the color is unusual. However, it is wise to let plumes develop fully, but watch that they do not pass their prime, losing color and turning yellow or brown. We usually harvest some in late July, although August and September are better. The best color and fullness comes on plants growing in sun on the south side of our gardens, but seedlings pop up in paths, in beds, even in the driveway, where they are certainly not wanted. We pick plumes from the unruly ones as early as possible and dry them in vases in the house. Here they develop full color.

Ambrosia becomes brittle with drying and shatters easily. After it is thoroughly dry, and before using it in wreaths and arrangements, put it in an open shed or sheltered spot where it can pick up some moisture. It may be treated with plastic spray but this destroys the scent.

Artemisia 'Silver King', *Artemisia albula*

This is the artemisia that is the basis of the wreaths and table trees described in chapters two and three. It does not grow readily from seed, so you will want to purchase at least six plants in spring to have an adequate harvest in fall. Full sun, good drainage, and space to spread are the three requirements. Artemisias grow rapidly into large clumps that need air and light. Every three years, plants should be divided. 'Silver King' grows to three feet, so set the plants at the back of your garden for a lovely cloud of white in summer, or choose some separate spot where they can spread unhindered.

Cut stalks in early autumn when seed-heads are pure white; if you wait too long, they may discolor or shatter. To get straight stiff pieces for dried arrangements, hang stalks upside-down in bunches, and let them dry out of the sun. Wreaths and trees are best made with freshly-cut, pliable artemisia, or with pieces laid in baskets to curve and curl as they dry. (Other useful artemisias include mugwort, tarragon, and wormwood, which are described below under these common names.)

Bedstraw, *Galium verum*

Our Lady's bedstraw, one of the manger herbs, was also considered a healing herb for fatigue, and it was used as a dye and for coloring butter. The lovely yellow blossoms, so sweet smelling in late June and early July, occur on thick matted plants that, once established, strangle weeds and grass and make a good groundcover. Start with two plants, set where they can spread. A sloping well-drained location where soil is lean and gravelly produces the best growth. Gather spikes in full color and hang in a dry place until they are thoroughly dried. Store carefully as they shatter easily. For the Advent Wreath, it is better to insert small rooted plants in the sphagnum moss.

Globe-amaranth, *Gomphrena globosa*

A symbol of eternity, this plant, once prominent at funerals and in churches, bears flowers that look like clover. With statice, tansy, and yarrow, it is our best source of natural color in the summer herb garden, for small winter arrangements, and for the Advent Wreath, where the purples and pinks look nice with any statice. It also makes a good accent in the Fragrant Wreath, and two or three of the conelike flowers will add interest to little baskets of dried herbs. Once dried, globe-amaranth does not lose color, which may be white, deep purple, or tones of pale pink to red.

Grow the eight- to eighteen-inch annual (I prefer larger types), from seed sown in flats in late March, preferably in a greenhouse. Lacking this, try to buy flats of seedlings at outdoor-planting time. Full sun is essential for good growth and flower production, dampness to be avoided. Snip individual blossoms as they open. Don't cut the entire plant. Hang four to eight flower-heads upside-down in a dry spot. Stems are weak but stiffen with hanging.

Hops, *Humulus lupulus*

Native to the British Isles and once used by the Romans as a pot herb, hops were not brewed for beer in England until the sixteenth century; this use came in with the Dutch. Our gift is a very old-fashioned one, a hop pillow, used to bring on sleep and to relieve ear- or tooth-ache. Hops contain lupulin, a golden dust that acts as a gentle sedative. We like hops for teas but alone it makes such a bitter brew that we mix it with China tea. Once leaves were sold for spring tonics.

To start a vine, obtain a root from a large specimen. Plant in full sun where soil is well drained. Dig a deep hole and prepare it with well-rotted manure and good compost. It takes three years for a vine to get large enough to cover fence or wall or to run up a tall pole. Hops need plenty of phosphate and nitrogen. To keep leaves green, spray for spider mites early in the growing season. However, when blossoms form, leaves naturally turn yellow and fall. As soon as the conelike blossoms, called catkins or strobiles, are fully formed, they turn an amber hue. For dried arrangements, pick while they are green. Hang in bunches in a warm place, out of the sun, where air freely circulates. Hops cure quickly.

Horehound, *Marrubium vulgare*

For frosty-leaved rosettes in wreaths and table decorations, or for flavoring candy or tea, this "bitter herb," associated with the Passover Feast, is one to grow in your garden. A favorite in folk remedies for coughs and colds, horehound was brought to America by the first settlers.

Sow seed early in spring in sandy soil with good drainage and in full sun. Seed germinates slowly, but some nicely-formed rosettes will be ready for your Christmas projects. The plant grows to three feet with wrinkled, almost white leaves. Horehound is perennial but better treated as biennial. Sow some seed every year, or divide large clumps in spring. Watch for seedlings, horehound readily naturalizes.

The thick leaves need to go through three rinses before they are ready for drying—first a warm-water bath, then two cool baths. Finally drain on a screen in the sink. Do the washing quickly or flavor will be lost. Dry out horehound leaves by hanging them in bunches in a warm dry place for a day or two. You can gather the fresh rosettes for decorations even after frost or when plants are covered with snow. Leaves hold form and color in spite of cold.

Lamb's-ears, *Stachys lanata*

This gray two-foot perennial, with velvety long-lasting leaves that beautifully frame the flower, is a pleasure in the garden and an effective accent in living wreaths as well as in any of the dried wreaths. In the past its use was largely medicinal. Lamb's-ears set no seed that you can depend upon but plants self-sow to some extent and side roots can be pulled and planted separately. Two to four plants soon become a border in any dry, well-drained area with full sun. Avoid excessive moisture, one of the few causes of loss.

For decorations, remove whole rosettes of leaves with some stem attached to hold them together. For the living wreaths, lift rooted plants; they will grow long after the holidays are over.

Lavender-cotton, *Santolina chamaecyparissus*

One of the grayist of plants, this lacy evergreen shrub may be grown as a neat hedge or allowed to spread. It is beautiful *along* a stone wall or planted directly *in* a wall where it showers down in a great foaming white cascade. At Christmas, we like the long-lasting gray foliage for living wreaths, we include it in the Advent Wreath, and also add it to our Herbal Christmas Tree.

Since there is apparently no viable seed available, start with cuttings or divisions of large plants. Or increase stands by layering. Sun, lime, and good drainage in a dry area are essential. Plants languish in moist places and humid weather. Give some winter cover, salt hay or hemlock boughs.

Green santolina, *S. viridis,* is a fine hardy perennial that grows to three feet. If given space, sun, and air around it, it can be used as an important symmetrical garden accent. In general, the same culture is required, though this green santolina does reasonably well in part shade. It has a strong resinous smell. On this account, we often substitute it for juniper in Christmas wreaths. It also adds a brilliant note of green to the Living Herb Tree and to kissing balls.

Lavender, *Lavandula officinalis*

The clean fresh scent of lavender has made it a popular herb since the time of the Greeks and Romans. It is hardy, undemanding, and requires only sun, sweet (alkaline) soil, and good drainage. Start lavender from small plants or from cuttings rooted in sand. It grows very slowly from seed that germinates best when sown early in spring, in March, or late in fall, in November. It may also be sown indoors in fall and grown under lights. This perennial herb grows one to three feet high and has fragrant gray-green velvety leaves. Flowers are small, set on spikes, and in shades of light and dark purple and pink, also white.

Harvest the blossoms for potpourris, sachets, and other scented gifts. Pick when fully open or just before the last florets unfold. Since the flowers contain little moisture, they dry easily when stems are placed in a vase or basket without water. Our Lavender Tree, made with both foliage and flowers on an artemisia-wrapped wire frame, is described in chapter two. Cuttings go into the Living Herb Tree and the Advent Wreath, and dried blossoms in the Victorian and Lavender wreaths.

Lemon balm, *Melissa officinalis*

A hardy perennial with lemon-scented leaves, this herb grows well in any soil in a well-drained spot with sun half the day, or even in shade. It may be started from seed sown in early spring or late fall. While seed is slow to germinate, plants, once started, grow quickly to a height of one to two feet. Frequent cutting keeps them under control. After you harvest the leaves, rinse once in cool water, then drain and dry for potpourris or teas. While fresh, they can be added to punch, fruit compote, or used as a garnish. Lemon balm is also attractive in arrangements.

Lemon verbena, *Lippia citriodora*

This herb is really a tropical tree, native to Guatemala and mountainous parts of South America. A tender perennial, unpruned, it may reach to ten feet, and in North America grows best in a tub that can be brought indoors in winter. Buy plants—four will yield an abundant harvest of fragrant leaves—and grow in sun or partial shade in rich soil with a good amount of well-rotted manure worked in. Also apply liquid plant food through the growing period, late winter through summer. Bring plants indoors well before frost and place at a sunny window. They may lose their leaves and stay dormant in winter, but will put out new growth in February and March when you take them outdoors again. Or you can store plants in winter in a cool light place, such as a basement with windows.

For fragrant gifts, potpourris, and a delicate lemon-flavored tea, collect leaves before they fall. Rinse once in cool water and drain on a screen. Then spread on a tray to dry before you pack in jars with tight lids.

Marjoram, *Origanum vulgare*

The perennial orégano that we grow for the sweet odors of both leaves and dried blossoms have little of the flavor of the Greek import, rather they suggest mint, which is their family. Plants grow from one to three feet with woolly leaves; blossoms are white, pale lavender, or dark bright pink. These extremely hardy plants self-sow freely enough to over-run your garden if you let them. They thrive in full sun but will live almost anywhere. Cut blossoms in various stages, harvesting the greatest number when they are pink and green, but do pick some after they turn rich brown. They are still fragrant then and make effective accents in wreaths, swags, and arrangements. This is the pot marjoram.

Mint, *Mentha*

Popular and easy perennials, mints come in other flavors beside the familiar spearmint. For teas, jellies, sauces, and candies, I like the fragrant orange mint, *Mentha citrata,* also called bergamot-mint; apple mint, *Mentha rotundifolia,* a tall, fuzzy variety; peppermint, *Mentha piperita;* and various spearmints, *Mentha spicata,* and curly mint, *Mentha crispa.* Mints thrive in rich moist soil, preferably in shade, but most kinds will grow well enough in lean soil and sun, too. Buy plants or rooted cuttings. Don't try to grow mints from seed. They multiply readily from roots, sending out runners that need to be controlled several times a year if mint is included in the garden. It is easier if you plant mints where they can spread and not over-run other herbs.

Cut mint often, from June on, to discourage the few pests that might eat leaves, and to have a sufficient supply for teas. To keep flavor and color, wash carefully and hang in bunches to dry quickly in a warm place out of the sun. When they are well dried, store mint leaves in airtight tins or large plastic bags away from the light.

Mugwort (beifuss), *Artemisia vulgaris*

In the Middle Ages, this was considered the plant of the weary traveler for it was reputed to allay fatigue. It is also known as the plant of Saint John. We use it in our dried arrangement in Saint Nicholas's shoe as a symbol for Black Peter who walked behind the Saint. The English used mugwort to flavor ale—hence the name—and in Germany it is traditional in stuffing for the Christmas goose. The silver-backed cut leaves and handsome seed-heads look well in almost all autumn and Christmas designs. We make attractive wreaths of it for midsummer.

One plant will suffice, and it is advisable to buy this. Handle it as you would a hardy shrub. It grows to four or five feet, and you will need to cut away many roots and seedlings each year to keep it under control. A sunny location is preferred. Transplanted, it grows well the first year but it is in its second and third years that you will have plenty to cut.

For Christmas decorations, wait to harvest until seed-heads form; they are gray and brown and make interesting finials for tall arrangements. Plants mature from August through fall, depending upon age and weather. Let stalks dry in a vase with other artemisias and a central motif of tansy. The stem is **woody and** does not need hanging to stiffen it.

Myrtle, *Myrtus communis*

This is one of the world's most venerated plants. Its tiny fragrant leaves were used in the Jewish feasts of the tabernacle; it symbolized the highest good, and love and domestic happiness in the home. It was the plant of the bride's crown signifying virtue. True myrtle, sometimes called Swedish myrtle, grows as a small tree or large shrub along Mediterranean shores, the small, pointed, shining leaves thickly set and emitting a wonderful camphorous odor when brushed. The blossoms, which appear on mature plants, are small, white, and delightful.

Purchase young plants, pot them in humusy soil, and repot as growth indicates. Set plants outdoors in summer; they do well in partial shade. Be sure to bring them in well before frost. They prefer a cool greenhouse and they must have such winter protection or they will die. We use myrtle in kissing balls, wreaths, and garlands to twine around our tall church candles, and include it in the Herbal Tree and the wreath that circles the punch bowl.

Pennyroyal, *Mentha pulegium*

This small-leaved creeping mint was once famous for curative teas. It was also considered death to insects as its name "flea away" implies. Pennyroyal is a tender perennial that may be grown from seed of excellent germination, or seeds may be left on plants to scatter and produce new ones. It likes lean soil, rocks, and sand, and grows well in shade. Attractive purple blossoms rise from prostrate growth, but it is the leaf that has the penetrating and pleasant scent. As a pot plant, pennyroyal will fill a basket or trail like a vine over the edge of a windowbox. We use rooted pieces in our living wreaths and put a plant of it in the manger scene.

Rosemary, *Rosmarinus officinalis*

Featured in legends and long associated with remembrance, rosemary is an essential Christmas herb. We use it, dried and fresh, in wreaths, in manger scenes and tableaux, in pomanders and gifts, in wassails, on roasts and in jellies and teas. A tender perennial with gray-green needle leaves, it eventually reaches three to five feet. Seed is slow to germinate and in most localities must be sown by May first. When seedlings are two inches high, transfer them to small pots in which they will develop strong roots. To speed growth, give plants liquid fertilizer, water daily, and mist leaves. As soon as pots are filled with roots, transfer plants to a sunny garden spot where soil is alkaline, moist, but well drained. Fertilize several times through the growing season. You can also propagate from cuttings. Root four- to six-inch pieces in vermiculite or sand. Keep well watered. In about five weeks, you can pot the rooted cuttings or set them out in your garden.

For decorations, rinse leaves in cool water, drain, and spread out on trays to dry. Since needles are sharp if left whole, for seasonings, teas, and jams, I run some through a coffee mill. In the

Herb-and-Spice Wreath, I use freshly-cut sprays and insert them while green.

Rue, *Ruta graveolens*

This blue-green herb, the rue of legends, makes a two- to three-foot shrub that is attractive in the garden even in winter. Since it holds colorful leaves long after Christmas, it is also fine for fall and winter arrangements. Rue was often tied in pomanders as protection against evil, and being a symbol of virtue and virginity, it was placed with rosemary around statues of the Virgin. Rue grows readily from seed but requires two years to make enough growth for cutting. It is best to buy plants, which will thrive in a hot dry place, be disease-free, and self-sow liberally.

Cut the green rosettes for Advent wreaths and also some long pieces for swags. Rue stays fresh for weeks. Include some in decorations for the Lucia Festival, since rue was held to be the plant of vision and Saint Lucy is patron of those with eye afflictions. Gather seed pods when they are an attractive yellow-green hue or after they turn brown. There is no need to dry them as they almost dry themselves on the plant. They look like Oriental hand-carved beads and are distinctive for dried wreaths.

Sage, *Salvia officinalis*

We use sage primarily as a seasoning, but as a symbol of health, immortality, and domestic happiness, we place it in our Advent and ivy wreaths and in our Living Herb Tree. A hardy perennial that reaches three feet, sage is easy to grow from seed planted in fertile, well-drained soil in a sunny location. Spring sowing will produce good cuttings by fall. Divide established plants to increase your supply.

To harvest, trim, but do not cut stalks to the ground. Rinse leaves in three waters—a warm bath followed by two cool ones. Do this quickly, drain on a screen in the sink, then hang bunches to dry. Don't strip off leaves until you are ready to bottle or use them—they keep better if left on the stems.

Statice, *Statice sinuata* and *S. maritima*

Statice, both annual and perennial, offers flowers of beautiful texture and colors; *S. sinuata,* the annual, comes from seed sown very early in spring, preferably in a greenhouse, or you can buy flats of seedlings. Transplant to your sunny garden when frost danger is passed, about May fifteenth. Cut stalks when flowers are fully open, but don't cut down the plant for blooming continues until just before frost. Hang in bunches to dry overnight. Statice does not fade and is a fine source of permanent pinks and purples.

Sea-statice, bog-rosemary, and sea-lavender are names applied to the wild perennial *S. maritima* of the marshes, whose long fleshy root, processed and powdered, was once used as an astringent. This is a decorative plant but we no longer try to grow it ourselves, for this rocky hillside is not right for plants that thrive only in wet places. The tiny blossoms on strong stems lose their lavender tint and dry out in thick clusters of little white stars. Those of us who view with horror the trend toward artificial materials, particularly value this plant. In the making of the Fragrant Wreath and the Herb-and-Spice Wreath, we combine it with artemisia. Outside, it withstands wind and damp weather and here at Caprilands turns our green Bird Tree into a snowy wonder.

Sweet Woodruff, *Asperula odorata*

Grow enough of this modest little perennial ground-cover so you can bottle fresh sprigs in white wine for the traditional May Day festival or use it to flavor a choice wine jelly. Dried woodruff leaves smell like fresh-cut hay, and we combine them with other fragrant leaves in potpourris. (Recipes are given in the next chapter.)

Grow woodruff in a sheltered spot under shrubs or trees in moist acid soil with peatmoss or leafmold added. It hardly reaches six inches and spreads nicely to form a lovely green carpet with a mossy smell. Buy plants or obtain cuttings from friends; seed rarely germinates and, when it does, takes two years. Woodruff needs to be trimmed regularly, especially during hot humid weather, to let air reach the lowest leaves. Don't cut foliage too close to the ground. For use, rinse cuttings briefly in cool water. Then spread them out to cure on a tray in a dry shaded place.

Tansy, *Tanacetum vulgare*

In our Christmas gifts, decorations, and dried arrangements, we use quantities of golden tansy blossoms. Although plants are fast growers and spread like weeds, we never seem to have enough. Luckily, tansy grows along roadsides throughout New England, so we can easily add to our home-supply when necessary. It is reputed to keep away moths, ants, flies, and such.

Tansy is a two- to four-foot perennial with aromatic ferny leaves and tight yellow, buttonlike flowers that grow in clusters. The feathery texture of tansy makes it a pleasant background for lower-growing herbs. Start tansy along a fence or garage where it will get full sun and some protection from wind and rain. Almost any soil will do if there is fair drainage. Seed is slow to germinate so you may want to buy some plants. Once started, tansy spreads rapidly.

Harvest with care. Wait until the florets are fully developed; if picked too early, they shrivel and may turn brown. Use them for colorful fragrant everlastings in the artemisia-based wreaths, described in chapter three. Or tuck blossoming sprays in little gift baskets of dried herbs and blossoms. The leaves, hung in bunches to dry are also used in a spicy mixture for storing woolens and furs (as described in the next chapter), or placed in an open bowl as a refreshing scent for a room.

Tarragon, *Artemisia dracunculus*

For the tarragon-flavored gifts from your kitchen and for fragrant potpourris (both described in the next chapter), you will want at least one large clump or two smaller plants in your garden. Select only true French tarragon; any other is all but flavorless. This one- to three-foot perennial grows only by root division, not from seed. Give it full sun at least half the day, good drainage, and some fertilizer each year. Divide plants every three years and cut them back frequently during the summer. Rinse cuttings quickly in cool water and hang them upside down in a dry shaded place. Use fresh cuttings for vinegars and tarragon jelly, dried leaves for seasonings.

Teasel, *Dipsacus*

Spiny-headed teasels provide a distinctive form for Christmas wreaths and swags, and they are a handsome addition to dried arrangements. Spray or gild them for a festive look. Because it holds up well in bad weather, teasel is excellent for outdoor decorations—all good reasons for including it in your Christmas garden.

Teasels are two- to six-foot biennials; seed sown one spring will not produce plants of any size until the next spring. Since seed is not generally available, purchase a few plants. Once started, teasels are self-sowing, and produce a good supply for many years. For large heads, *D. pullonum* is a good variety; for arrangements, I also like the smaller wild plant, *D. sylvestris*. Plant teasels in almost any soil where they will get full sun. Although they are not exacting, I notice that my finest stand grows next to, and in, the compost heap. To harvest, simply let these thistles stand uncut in the garden until the seeds fall. Then trim the stalks for use in Christmas designs.

English wool merchants brought teasels to New York State in the eighteenth century; they were used originally to comb yarn and "tease" cloth. The name comes from the Saxon word, *taesan*. Teasels are also called brushes-and-combs and church-broom, names that tell of other uses.

Thyme, *Thymus vulgaris*

A manger herb, thyme is included in our nativity scenes along with rosemary, bedstraw, and pennyroyal. We also use the fragrant cuttings in our living wreaths and trees, and the lovely blossoms in dried wreaths. Beside its traditional association with meats and poultry, thyme brings an unusual flavor to the grape jelly we make for Christmas presents.

The most decorative and long-lasting types are Broadleaf English and Narrowleaf French—both strains of the common or culinary *T. vulgaris*. The creeping four- to six-inch varieties of mother-of-thyme are better suited to garden paths and slopes. Lemon thymes have fascinating scents and make good teas.

Thyme needs good drainage, a half day of sun or open filtered shade, and a sweet soil. To assure alkalinity, mix in a little lime when you plant. You can start common thyme from seeds, but plants develop slowly, so you may prefer to start your Christmas garden with a few established plants. Growing only twelve inches high, they make attractive borders for paths or beds. Although they are root-hardy, thymes come through northern winters better when protected with salt hay or evergreen boughs. Don't trim plants too close when harvesting; in fall leave about three inches of growth above ground.

For fragrant wreaths, gather blossoming sprays in May or June. For seasonings, trim plants through summer and fall, preferably before they bloom again. Rinse leaves quickly three times—warm water followed by cool. Let drain, then heap on a basket or tray. Since the leaves hold little moisture, you can dry a whole basketful in any place that is out of the sun and not damp. (Humidity is harmful.) When leaves are fully dry, strip the stems, and bottle right away in jars with tight lids. Store in a closed cupboard.

Wormwood, *Artemisia absinthium*

This plant, true wormwood, with blue-gray leaves, which look like those of the chrysanthemum, is attractive in the garden and also lovely for autumn and early Christmas bouquets and decorations. A leaf may be added to a swizzle or a punch but, judiciously, for wormwood is potent and bitter. It gives a tang to absinthe and to "bitters." Wormwood is an essential ingredient in our Herbal Moth Preventive. Its reputation for driving away moths, fleas, and all vermin is well documented in herbals of the fourteenth century. It was also used in salves for the sprains and bruises of man and beast.

Plants will grow from seed, but it takes two years to get a good-sized, four-foot clump. If you buy plants, two will be adequate, for they scatter seed that yields new plants large enough for cutting the next year. Wormwood is not demanding as to soil but grows larger when this is fertile and in full sun or partial shade with good drainage. In August and September, we harvest the spirelike stalks of brown seeds in gray cases and dry them, like mugwort, right in the vase. They make interesting finials and are shapely for line arrangements.

Yarrow, *Achillea*

Invaluable for golden color in dried arrangements and in artemisia-based wreaths and trees, yarrow has been an important herb through the years. Achilles is said to have used it to stop the bleeding wounds of his soldiers, and for centuries it has been carried in battle because of its magical as well as medicinal properties.

Yarrow is a hardy perennial. Set out a row of husky plants where they can multiply freely; you can divide them at the end of the second year. Sun, soil sweetened with lime, good drainage, and a generous spread of compost will produce handsome flowers. Grow plenty of yarrow since it is not easy to buy. For shades from pale cream to deepest gold, plant *A. filipendulina* and its varieties; these grow from four to five feet.

The white-flowered wild yarrow or milfoil, *A. millefolium,* grows to two feet. The one-foot woolly dwarf yarrows, *A. tomentosum,* with short-stemmed, flat, yellow blooms and ferny leaves make good ground-covers. Pick flowers in early June through July before they shatter. Hang stems upside down in bunches of six to twelve in a dry airy place. Yarrow blooms are so durable you can even use them on outside wreaths at Christmastime.

> *Come into the Christmas garden*
> *That groweth all the year,*
> *And makes perfumes*
> *For all your rooms*
> *And herbs for yuletide cheer.*—A.G.S.

12
Herbal Gifts
from Kitchen and Garden

Here are gifts to make from the many fine herbs growing in your Christmas garden: candied mint leaves, distinctive herb-flavored jellies, vinegars, and teas—for any number of herbs lend refreshing flavor to the teapot—fragrant potpourris, pomanders, an aromatic pillow for insomnia, a rag doll, and baskets of sweet-smelling lavender. Of course, to any friend who enjoys cooking, a package or two of your own home-grown herbs is a welcome gift, indeed.

An old-fashioned rag doll made fragrant with a stuffing of dried lavender.

10"

GIFTS FROM THE KITCHEN

HERBAL TEAS

Interest in herbal teas increases every year and at Caprilands we experiment with different combinations. Our favorite tea includes various mints with other herbs for a good-tasting brew. And this is rich in herbal symbolism—mint for wisdom, thyme for bravery, calendulas for the complexion and disposition, rosemary for memory, camomile for quiet sleep, and sage for immortality.

CAPRILANDS TEA

6 cups dried shredded apple-mint leaves
2 cups mixed dried shredded mint leaves
1 cup dried lemon-verbena leaves

1 cup dried calendula blossoms
½ cup dried rosemary
¼ cup dried thyme
1 cup dried sage

Mix leaves and blossoms together and store in airtight cannisters. To brew, use 1 teaspoon for each cup of boiling water, and allow at least 10 minutes for full flavor to develop. This mixture may also be used along with your favorite Oriental tea. Add a tablespoon to a 6-cup pot of any standard blend of tea.

ORANGE-MINT TEA

This fragrant, spicy combination is made with Oriental tea. Use the coarse blade of a food chopper to grind the orange peel or dry it well, then crush in mortar and pestle.

6 cups dried orange-mint leaves
2 cups dried apple-mint leaves
1 cup dried coarsely-ground orange peel

1 cup black Oriental tea
½ cup whole cloves

PEPPERMINT AND SPEARMINT TEAS

These mints are strongly flavored and are usually best brewed without other herbs. After the leaves are well dried, crumble them and package for gifts in jars or tins with tight-fitting lids. Label and give this advice on your gift card: Measure 1 spoonful to 1 cup of boiling water, and let stand for at least 10 minutes. Make this in a teapot to keep it hot.

ROSEMARY TEA

Reputed to restore memory, rosemary makes a distinctive tea. Infuse the dried needles for 15 minutes, allowing a good teaspoonful for each cup of boiling water.

LEMON TEA

Combine 1 cup of dried crumbled leaves of lemon balm with 1 cup of dried lemon verbena. Cut the yellow peel from 2 lemons, dry it out, then grind it, and mix in with the leaves. Pack in apothecary jars with tight lids. This mixture combines deliciously with any good Oriental tea and is also refreshing brewed on its own. Allow a heaping teaspoonful to a cup; it takes about 15 minutes for full flavor to develop.

MINT SAUCE

A traditional seasoning for lamb, this sauce is also a welcome addition to fruit salads. For gift-giving make a large batch. Shred 2 cups of fresh spearmint leaves, crush in a bowl with ½ cup of sugar. Add 1 teaspoon of salt, and pour in 1 quart of white malt vinegar. Beat well. Pour into a saucepan and boil for 10 minutes. Let cool, then strain and bottle in small quantities, with a little fresh mint in each container. Label and give some suggestions for use.

ROSEMARY JELLY

4 cups cranberry juice, *or* 2 cups cranberry juice and 2 cups apple juice
12 sprigs (1 cup) fresh rosemary
8 cups sugar

2 cinnamon sticks, 4 inches long
6 whole cloves
½ cup chopped candied lemon and orange peel
2 6-ounce bottles pectin

Boil juice with rosemary sprigs for about 15 minutes. Stir in sugar and bring to a boil again. Break up cinnamon sticks and add to juice with cloves and peel. Add the pectin and boil 1 minute, or according to directions on the bottle. Then pour into hot sterilized jars. Makes 12 to 15 four-ounce jars.

SWEET WOODRUFF WINE JELLY

2 cups Christmas May Wine (see recipe below)
4 cups sugar

1 6-ounce bottle pectin
12 sprigs fresh woodruff
Extra woodruff sprigs

Prepare the wine according to the recipe. Bring to a boil and let boil 1 minute. Add sugar, return to boiling, and pour in pectin. Cook at a rolling boil for 1 minute. Strain out leaves if they have darkened. Pour into sterilized jars and put one or two fresh sprigs of woodruff in each. Makes 6 to 8 four-ounce jars.

TARRAGON JELLY

1 quart sweet cider
½ cup vinegar
12 fresh tarragon sprigs, 8 inches long

8 cups sugar
4 drops yellow food coloring
2 6-ounce bottles pectin
Extra sprigs of tarragon

In a large saucepan, boil together cider, vinegar, and the 12 tarragon sprigs for 15 minutes. Stir in sugar and food coloring, and let come to boiling again. Pour in pectin and allow to boil 1 minute. Place small sprigs of fresh tarragon in each hot sterilized jar, pour in mixture, screw on lids, and turn upside down until jelly has partially set. Turn right-side-up, remove lid, pour paraffin over jelly. Label and store until Christmas. Makes 12 to 15 four-ounce jars.

THYME GRAPE JELLY

Originally this jelly was made with wild grapes, but if they are unavailable, prepared grape juice, though less romantic, tastes almost as delicious.

4 cups grape juice
10 sprigs fresh thyme, 3 inches long
1 lemon, sliced not peeled
1 orange, quartered not peeled

4 whole cloves
8 cups sugar
½ cup raisins
1 6-ounce bottle pectin
Extra sprigs of thyme

Boil grape juice with the 10 sprigs of thyme for 10 minutes. Add lemon slices and orange sections, cloves, and sugar. Cook until fruit is tender, about 15 minutes. Lift out fruit, cool, then grind it, and return to the liquid. Stir in raisins. Bring to boiling, pour in pectin, and boil 1 minute. Skim. Pour into sterilized jars, adding a fresh sprig of thyme to each. Makes 12 to 15 four-ounce jars.

MINT JELLY

6 cups apple juice
½ cup cider vinegar
4 cups fresh spearmint leaves, crushed
12 cups sugar

2 6-ounce bottles pectin
1 teaspoon mint flavoring
Green vegetable coloring
Extra mint sprigs

Boil together the apple juice, vinegar, and mint leaves for 15 minutes. Stir in sugar and bring to a boil. Add pectin, boil 1 minute, or according to directions on the bottle. Strain; add mint flavoring and coloring. Then pour into sterilized jars, placing a fresh sprig of mint in each jar. Makes 15 to 20 four-ounce jars.

MINT VINEGAR

A distinctive addition to salads, cocktail spreads, and sauces, this vinegar in compresses also soothes an aching head. To a gallon of white or cider vinegar, add 8 cups of crushed fresh mint leaves. Let stand one month or longer. Strain into decorative bottles, place a fresh spray of mint in each, and label.

TARRAGON VINEGAR

One of the first herbs to harvest from your Christmas garden is tarragon. By midsummer, you can cut pieces 8 to 10 inches long. To flavor a gallon of red-wine vinegar, cut a dozen pieces, rinse quickly, and gently pat dry between towels. Put the tarragon in the wine vinegar, cork the jug, and set aside in a warm place for at least a month. If you wait until October, the flavor will be even better. For gifts, pour vinegar into small bottles with a fresh sprig of tarragon in each.

A TARRAGON GIFT BASKET

Dried tarragon for seasoning is a welcome kitchen gift. When the herb is chip-dry, remove leaves from stems and crumble but do not powder. (Powdering releases essential oils and reduces flavor.) Put in glass jars or painted tins, and label. To make the gift special, select one or two favorite recipes that use tarragon. In an herb-gathering basket, place a jar of dried tarragon, a bottle of Tarragon Vinegar, and the recipes. Tie green nylon net over the basket and finish with a bright red bow.

POULTRY SEASONING

Sage is one of the principle ingredients in this seasoning which combines with other herbs to produce an unusual flavor. Since sage carries a wish for health, youthfulness, and immortality, it makes a most fitting Christmas gift. The saying is, "He that would live for aye must eat sage in May," but why wait? Sage also represents domestic happiness, and should please a friend who enjoys cooking.

2 cups dried parsley	1 teaspoon dried onion powder
1 cup dried crumbled sage	2 tablespoons salt
½ cup ground rosemary	1 teaspoon freshly-ground pepper
¼ cup ground marjoram	½ teaspoon ground ginger

Combine herbs and seasonings and place small amounts in jars or cellophane bags. Give the direction to add 1 tablespoon of the seasoning to ¼ pound of butter to rub over chicken, turkey, or goose before cooking.

CANDIED MINT LEAVES

Select perfectly-shaped leaves of young apple mint. Whip the white of an egg until it is no longer slippery but not frothy either. With a small camel's-hair brush, paint leaves lightly with the egg white—or dip them. Sprinkle with superfine sugar, allowing green of leaves to show through. Line a tray with waxed paper. Place the leaves on the tray and set it on the open door of a slow oven. When mint leaves are dry, store them carefully in a tin or jar to prevent breakage. These candied leaves embellish a cake handsomely and can also be served on sherbet and fruit compotes. Try them with a cup of tea or serve them in a candy dish. Or use them in decorative designs with candied violets or roses.

OLD-FASHIONED HOREHOUND CANDY

This candy has a bittersweet flavor, and it is not to everyone's taste, but to some it has delightful flavor that recalls childhood joys. Those who like horehound have a real passion for it.

3 quarts water
1 ounce (¼ cup) dried horehound
   leaves, flowers, and stems
3 cups brown sugar
1 teaspoon cream of tartar

¼ cup rum, *or* 1 teaspoon lemon
   juice
1 teaspoon butter
Superfine sugar

Bring water to a boil. Remove from heat, add horehound, and let steep for 30 minutes. Strain and let settle. For each batch of candy, pour 2½ cups of liquid into a heavy saucepan. To it add sugar, cream of tartar, rum or lemon juice, and bring to boiling. When syrup reaches 240 degrees, add the butter. Continue boiling without stirring until syrup reaches 312 degrees. Pour into a shallow buttered pan. Let cool until you can handle, then shape into small candies, roll in superfine sugar, wrap each one in waxed paper, and pack in decorative tins. Makes about 25 candies.

CHRISTMAS MAY WINE

A unique and welcome gift that looks ahead to spring is a bottle of dry sauterne or Rhine wine delicately flavored with sweet woodruff. Make this in summer when you trim the woodruff plants.

For each gallon of wine, add 1 cup (packed) of fresh woodruff leaves. Let them stand in the wine at least three days, but preferably for a month. Pour wine into quart bottles, place a few fresh green woodruff sprigs in each, and cork well. Wrap each bottle in clear plastic, tie with a bunch of woodruff sprigs, and attach a card with the May Bowl recipe below. You can flavor brandy with woodruff, too, and use it in the May Bowl. Store wine bottles for Christmas-giving on their sides in a cool dark place.

MAY BOWL—*WALDMEISTER* OR *MAI TRANK*

1 quart whole strawberries	1 cup brandy
1 cup sugar	1 quart champagne (optional)
1 pint crushed strawberries	Woodruff sprigs
1 gallon dry sauterne	Violets
1 quart Christmas May Wine (above)	

Over the whole berries, sprinkle ½ cup sugar. Add ½ cup sugar to the crushed berries, and put the fruit in a refrigerator. At serving time, chill a large punch bowl (if glass, place two silver spoons in the bottom to prevent cracking; remove spoons before serving). Place a cake of ice in the bowl, pour the crushed sugared berries over the ice. Add sauterne, the Christmas May Wine, brandy, and champagne if using. Garnish the bowl with the whole strawberries, fresh woodruff, and violets. When serving, put a whole berry in each cup. Serves 12 adequately.

FRAGRANT GIFTS FROM THE GARDEN

In the dooryard garden, we grow the fragrant plants from which we make potpourris, sachets, and other scented gifts. Much prized are French and lemon thymes, lavender, sweet alyssum, orange and pineapple mints, and many scented geraniums, including 'Rober's Lemon Rose', 'Dr. Livingston' or 'Skeleton Rose', old-fashioned rose (*Pelargonium graveolens*), lemon (*P. crispum* and *P. limoneum*), coconut (*P. grossularioides*), and the pungent pheasant's-foot (*P. glutinosum*), as well as apple, nutmeg, 'Old Spice', and the incense-smelling, oak-leaved types.

Rosemary, fragrant white and purple heliotrope, true myrtle, jasmine, pineapple sage, and plants of bay flourish with African baby's-breath (*Chaenostoma fastigiatum*), which provides white blooms all summer long. Shaded by the rosemary are beds of sweet woodruff, which when dried smells of vanilla and new-mown hay. Woodruff may be cut more than once in a season, and by November a good supply should be on hand for potpourris.

Ways to present lavender

FRAGRANT BASKETS. Miniature splint market baskets, 2 to 3 inches long, make appealing gifts when filled with sweet lavender flowers, the whole thing wrapped in net or organdy. For each basket, you need about 1½ cups of dried blossoms stripped from stalks. Cut pink, lavender, and purple organdy or net into double squares to hold the flowers. Place some blossoms on each square, gather edges together, and tie with lavender ribbon. Attach the ribbon to a basket handle and insert 12 flowering spikes in the bow. Package in transparent plastic.

LAVENDER SACHET. Make little sachets, about four, the size of a walnut, for each miniature basket. Combine ½ pound of lavender flowers in a bowl with ¼ pound powdered gum benzoin and 10 drops of oil of lavender. Wrap the mixture in a double layer of net, tie with ribbon, and add a sprig of lavender. For a more festive look, let ribbon trail over the edge of the basket.

BASKETS WITH BLOSSOMS.   Cover the bottom of a tiny basket with florist clay. Press in spikes of lavender until the basket is almost full. Then tuck in sprigs of flowering thyme, small white everlastings, and in center a floret of purple statice. To preserve fragrance, enclose the basket in clear plastic and close with a tie of purple ribbon.

SPRAYS OR SWAGS.   Dainty sprays or tiny decorative swags are simple to make. Take about 25 flowering lavender spikes, lay them flat, placing 12 on each side with stems facing the center of the swag. Bind stems together with light wire. Cover the center by wiring on sprigs of lavender leaves and a few sprigs of thyme and rosemary; tie on colorful ribbons. Let dry well before wrapping in plastic.

LAVENDER RAG DOLL.   A fragrant version of the old-fashioned rag doll could be a cherished gift for a child. To make the doll, cut and partly sew up the body from a piece of unbleached muslin. Partially fill with cotton batting. Next prepare the scent. Place 1 cup of dried lavender flowers in a bowl; on top, place 1 teaspoon granulated orris root, then add to it 2 drops of oil of lavender. Mix well and stuff into the cotton batting. Sew up the doll and make a dress of calico, also perhaps a gardening apron. Place a little basket of dried lavender in the doll's hand.

POMANDERS

The name pomander comes from the French *pomme* for apple, referring to the round shape of early scent balls, and amber from the fixative, ambergris. In time, *pomme d'ambre* became pomander. These spice balls, traditionally medicinal and worn to counteract odors, today are hung from ribbons in a room or closet or tucked into blanket chests or drawers to give an aromatic scent.

I sometimes make nosegays of artemisia, tansy flowers, and everlastings, and tie them into the ribbons on a pomander to give a friend who is ill. Pomanders bring welcome fragrance to a hospital room, where sweet flowery scents are sometimes cloying.

To make pomanders

Pomanders are made two ways: from fruit pulp, drained, spiced, and shaped; or from whole fruits studded with whole cloves and coated with powdered spices. For the pulp method, apple works well but I have also used quince pulp. The pulp that remains after jelly-making, is cleaned of seeds, drained, and pressed against a sieve until no liquid seeps through.

To each cup of well-drained pulp is added: 1 teaspoon ground cloves, ½ teaspoon ground nutmeg, ¼ teaspoon ground ginger, and 1 teaspoon powdered orris root. All this is well stirred. The pulp is then shaped into balls about the size of a walnut, and each ball is rolled in a mixture of ground cloves and cinnamon until it feels quite dry. (The pulp will absorb a fair amount of the spices.) At this point, if you wish, you can add a few drops of oil of cloves, patchouli or rose oil to each pomander.

After about an hour of drying, pomanders will be firm enough to pierce with a needle, and you can then draw a narrow ribbon or linen thread through them. Piercing, crosswise, three-quarter way down is more likely to prevent breakage than piercing straight through the center. After they are threaded, let the pomanders dry a little longer; then tie three to six of them in a cluster with a ribbon. Or to avoid piercing, which can break them, wrap each one in net or gold lace and tie at the top with a gold ribbon.

Less difficult to make are pomanders of whole fruits studded with cloves. Start with firm apples. It is easier to press clove

Pomanders. (Above) Fruit pulp is sieved, shaped into balls, dried, pierced with a needle, clustered, and suspended by a ribbon. (Below) Whole fruit is studded with cloves, rolled in a spice mixture, dried, and decorated with a ribbon for hanging.

stems into them, and for children, until they get the knack of it, apples are best to learn on. Other fruits, especially thin-skinned oranges and quinces are also good possibilities. Fruits of different sizes and shapes, and, of course, varying aromas are desirable if pomanders are to be hung in clusters. But my experience has been that crabapples tend to be dry, tangerines break easily, lemons and limes have very tough skins, and pears soften too quickly to be workable.

For 6 to 8 apples or oranges you will need:

½ pound whole long-stemmed cloves
1 cup (about) ground spices, including
¼ cup ground cinnamon
¼ cup ground cloves
¼ cup ground nutmeg and allspice
¼ teaspoon ground ginger
¼ cup powdered orris root

Select only sound fruits. Hold firmly, but do not squeeze; insert the whole cloves in close rows, but avoid placing too many in one spot as this may cause skin to break. Cloves need not touch if you roll the balls in a spice bath afterwards. Don't make holes for the cloves with a needle or other tool, for the cloves will fall out later if you do, and it doubles the time of making them.

After cloves are placed, roll your pomander in the spice mixture given above, coating it completely to keep out air. It is important to finish each pomander within twenty-four hours; it should only take you thirty minutes to sixty minutes for each one. Keep it in the open; do not cover.

Let pomanders remain in the spice mixture in an open bowl in a warm dry place for about a week. We place ours for a center-piece in a large copper vessel on the dining table, and the spicy aroma of curing pomanders penetrates the entire house. At the end of a week, the pomanders should be sufficiently hardened to tie up for gifts. However, they are still too fresh to store in airtight containers.

You may want to add an essence for lasting fragrance. For each orange or apple, allow about four drops of *one* of these oils: rose, patchouli, vetiver, clove, jasmine, sandalwood, bergamot, or orange blossom; for lemon pomanders, use oil of lemon verbena. These essences or oils are not to be confused with perfumes, which are diluted with alcohol. All oils smell very strong for the first few days; some, like patchouli, sandalwood, and vetiver are even rank, but they soon mellow and blend with the other scents.

Spice and fruit pomanders without oils will be fragrant for several years. When you find their aroma fading, wash your pomanders in warm water, roll them in a fresh spice bath, and add a drop or two of clove or cinnamon oil. Let them remain in the spices for a few days, then tie with fresh ribbons.

> *To me my Julia lately sent*
> *A Braclet richly Redolent:*
> *The Beads I kist, but most lov'd her*
> *That did perfume the Pomander.*—Robert Herrick

POTPOURRIS

We gather scented leaves through summer and late into fall for potpourri. As the leaves dry, we put them in individual airtight containers, label and store in a dry cool place until we have time to combine leaves with fixatives and perhaps with spices and essences. It is best to make potpourris well ahead of Christmas, so they may ripen about a month before being packaged in jars for gifts.

Fixatives, such as benzoin, tonka beans, and orris root hold fragrance in the leaves and also intensify it. Orris root should be granulated for potpourris, not powdered, for powder would give leaves a dusty look. Benzoin, a gum, should be crushed or ground to powder, and tonka beans should be ground. Chips of sandalwood are best for potpourris, and vetiver is supplied in granular form or as an oil.

Oils or essences are sometimes used. These are best introduced by placing the fixative, such as orris root, on top of leaves and petals, adding drops of oil on it, then stirring both through the leaves. We frequently include some dried scentless blossoms just for color when the potpourri is to be displayed in a glass jar or open bowl.

LEMON-VERBENA POTPOURRI

Place 2 cups of dried lemon-verbena leaves in a bowl. Mix in 1 cup dried lemon-balm leaves, the shredded petals of 6 dried calendulas, and ½ cup grated lemon peel. On top, put 2 teaspoons granulated orris root and then 2 drops of lemon-verbena oil. Stir all together. In a glass apothecary jar, press small dried marigolds against the glass for color, and then put in the potpourri mixture. When this is completely dry, close the jar and tie with a yellow and moss-green velvet bow. Lemon-geranium leaves also combine well with this mixture.

SPICY POTPOURRI

This aromatic mixture may also be burned as incense.

2 cups dried rose petals
1 cup dried lavender
1 cup frankincense "pebbles"
¼ cup myrrh "pebbles"
½ cup crushed benzoin
1 cup sandalwood chips
¼ cup ground tonka beans
1 cup cut vetiver
½ cup coarsely-ground cinnamon sticks

½ cup powdered cinnamon
½ cup powdered cloves
¼ cup powdered nutmeg
¼ cup ground allspice
¼ cup crushed coriander seeds
1 cup granulated orris root
20 drops oil of rose
4 drops oil of vetiver
4 drops oil of patchouli

In a large bowl, mix together petals, leaves, gums and spices. Place orris root on top; add drops of rose, vetiver, and patchouli oils. Stir through, allow to mellow a month in a tightly-closed container, turning leaves over from time to time. Then package for Christmas gifts.

SWEET WOODRUFF POTPOURRI I

This is a very fragrant subtle combination with no essence added; ingredients are simply mixed together.

> 2 cups dried woodruff leaves
> 1 cup dried shredded rose-geranium leaves
> 2 cups dried rose petals
> ½ cup sandalwood chips
> ½ cup granulated orris root
> 4 tonka beans, crushed or ground

SWEET WOODRUFF POTPOURRI II

> 2 cups dried woodruff leaves
> 1 cup dried lemon-verbena leaves
> 1 cup dried lemon-geranium leaves
> 1 cup dried calendula flowers
> ¼ cup granulated orris root
> 4 drops oil of lemon verbena

Combine dried leaves and flowers in a bowl. Place orris root on top, add drops of oil to it, then mix through. Store in glass jars with tight lids, decorate with small bunches of sweet woodruff that was hung to dry when green. Place in plastic bags and hold at least a month before Christmas.

HERB-GARDEN POTPOURRI

1 cup dried French thyme
1 cup dried lemon thyme
1 cup dried marjoram
2 cups dried rosemary
1 cup dried tarragon leaves
1 cup dried orégano
1 cup dried orange-mint leaves

1 cup dried rose-geranium leaves
2 cups dried rose petals
2 cups dried lavender flowers
¼ cup crushed coriander seeds
1 cup granulated orris root
Blossoms of orégano, bachelor's-buttons, larkspur, delphinium

POTPOURRI DE COLOGNE

We find this mixture as refreshing as the famous Eau de Cologne.

2 cups dried rose petals
2 cups finely-cut rosemary
Peel of 6 oranges, dried and finely ground
Peel of 4 lemons, dried and finely ground

¼ cup granulated orris root
10 drops oil of orange blossom
10 drops oil of bergamot
2 drops oil of rosemary

Combine petals, rosemary, and dried peel in a bowl. Place orris root on top. Drop oils onto the fixative and stir through.

> *Then, were not summer's distillations left,*
> *A liquid prisoner, pent in walls of glass,*
> *Beauty's effect with beauty were bereft,*
> *Nor it, nor no remembrance what it was;*
> *But flowers distilled, though they with winter meet,*
> *Leese but their show; their substance still lives sweet.*
> —Shakespeare

PILLOW OF HOPS

This comforting pillow has had the sanction of two English kings, George III and Edward VII. Hops contain lupulin, a golden dust that acts as a sedative. Collect the catkins when the hop vine blooms. Dry them well. Make a 6- by 8-inch inner case of unbleached muslin. Place hops inside and sew up. Make an outer covering, half an inch larger, of washable calico or toile, perhaps with a garden scene. Enclose a card with the pillow explaining its effectiveness against insomnia. It also eases tooth- and ear-ache, and is most helpful if heated. You might suggest using it with a heating pad.

HERBAL MOTH PREVENTIVE

For a different fragrance—one not so sweet as most potpourris —this excellent mixture offers a refreshing scent if placed in an open bowl in a room and stirred occasionally. It is effective against moths when stored with woolens and furs. To begin with, we hang green tansy from the kitchen rafters, along with sprays of wormwood, rue, southernwood, and rosemary. When they have dried, we strip off the brittle leaves and mix with various ingredients in these proportions:

6 cups dried tansy leaves	1 cup vetiver cuttings
2 cups dried wormwood leaves	½ cup granulated orris root
1 cup dried rue	6 drops oil of clove
½ cup ground spices (cinnamon, cloves, nutmeg)	6 drops oil of pine

Cut tansy leaves with shears and shred the other leaves. Mix with the spices and vetiver. Put the orris root on top, add the drops of oil to it, then mix well.

GIFTS IN BRIEF

Agrimony, *Agrimonia eupatoria*
   Ground leaves and dried blossoms make excellent herbal tea.
Ambrosia, *Chenopodium botrys*
   For gifts and wreaths, grow all you can.
Angelica, *Angelica archangelica*
   Candied stems for Christmas cakes; prepare small stems for angelica jelly or jam.
Bachelor's-buttons, *Centaurea cyanus*
   Dry the polka-dot type to give color to rose jars and potpourris.
Basil, *Ocimum basilicum*
   Make a basil vinegar, using purple-leaved basil for color; put a clove of garlic in some of the bottles; a gift for salad-makers.
Bay, *Laurus nobilis*
   Whole green leaves for the Herb-and-Spice Wreath; freshly-dried leaves for the cook.
Bedstraw, *Galium verum*
   A manger herb; also used in herbal baths.

Borage, *Borago officinalis*
Candy some of the bright blue flowers for cake decoration; dip freshly-cut blooms in beaten egg white, then in superfine sugar, and let dry.

Burnet, *Sanguisorba minor*
With cucumber flavor, delightful salad green for winter; nice hostess gift if mixed in cream cheese with chives for a spread. May also be used in vinegar.

Calendula, *Calendula officinalis* and other varieties
Dry blossoms for color in potpourris; also use as a tea, ½ teaspoon crushed flowers to a cup.

Camomile, *Anthemis nobilis*
Pick flower-heads and dry for camomile tea; package flowers for those with insomnia.

Caraway, *Carum carvi*
For flavoring applesauce, Christmas cookies, and breads; used in seed packages attached to kitchen wreaths.

Catnip, *Nepeta cataria*
For appreciative cats, to make a catnip mouse or ball, or a bouquet tied with ribbon for the tree.

Chervil, *Anthriscus cerefolium*
A valued gift for devotees of French cooking; dry the leaves, package, and label them.

Chives, *Allium schoenoprasum; A. tuberosum*
Give potted chives for a window garden; frozen or dried chives for seasoning. Garlic chives are fine for salads; use seeds in Seed-and-Sow Wreath.

Coriander, *Coriandrum sativum*
Give seeds for flavoring cookies and breads; also used in potpourris; in curry for Near Eastern cookery.

Costmary, *Chrysanthemum balsamita*
Give in a sachet for linens; press long leaves for bookmarks, known as Bible leaf.

Dill, *Anethum graveolens*
Called dill weed. Dry leaves, cut, and package for seasoning; make dill vinegar with a dill umbrel in each bottle.

Germander, *Teucrium lucidum*
Resembles boxwood, glossy dark green for herbal arrangements.

Lavender-cotton, *Santolina chamaecyparissus*
Cut for wreaths and table bouquets.

Lovage, *Levisticum officinale*
Celery-flavored leaves for seasoning; seeds for gardening friends.

Marjoram, *Origanum marjorana*
Commercial marjoram is seldom the sweet kind; true home-grown marjoram, dried for seasoning, will be appreciated by all cooks.

Rue, *Ruta graveolens*
Use in Saint Lucy ceremonies, as a charm, in wreaths and swags.

Scotch broom, *Cytisus scoparius*
Long green wands represent switches in the shoe arrangement for Saint Nicholas.

Shallots, *Allium cepa ascalonicum*
This delectable onion is a gift for gourmets; advise them to save a few for planting.

Southernwood, *Artemisia abrotanum*
For a lemon-and-camphor scent in moth preventives; tie in bunches with rosemary and tansy.

Summer savory, *Satureja hortensis*
Compatible with all bean dishes and hard to find among commercial seasonings. When chip-dry, pull leaves and store in bottles for gifts.

Violets and Violas, *Viola*
Candy the blossoms for cake decoration, adding a little essence of violet.

Index

Numbers in boldface type refer to illustrations.

ABOUT THE AUTHOR

Adelma Grenier Simmons, whose shop at "Caprilands" in Coventry, Connecticut, and booth at the International Flower Show attract a horde of herb and other garden enthusiasts, is a popular lecturer and a designer of authentic herb gardens for historical societies, museums, antique dealers, reconstructed villages like Storrowton, and flower shows featuring eighteenth-century gardens. Through the year, she gives lecture-luncheons at her home where guests always demand her marvelous recipes. Mrs. Simmons has an imaginative approach to cooking and decorating with herbs and is, indeed, one of the foremost authorities on this popular garden subject.